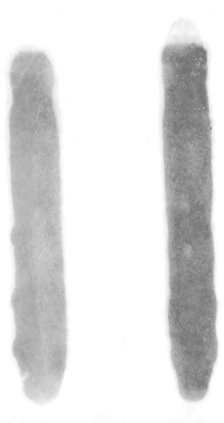

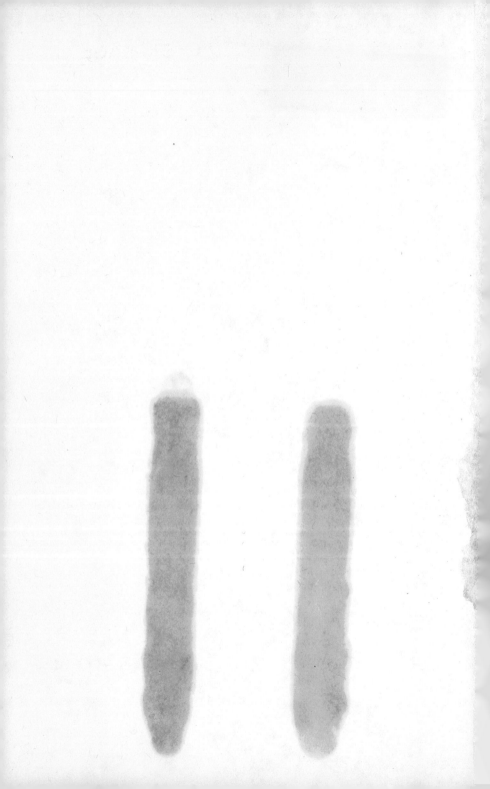

# RILKE: Nine Plays

RAINER MARIA

# RILKE

# Nine Plays

*Translated by Klaus Phillips and John Locke*

*Introduction by Klaus Phillips*

Cop. a

*Frederick Ungar Publishing Co.*

*New York*

*Library of Congress Cataloging in Publication Data*
*Rilke, Rainer Maria, 1875–1926.*
*Nine plays.*
*Bibliography: p.*
*CONTENTS: Murillo.—"Now and in the hour of our*
*death."—Early frost.—Air at high altitude.—Vigils.—*
*Not present.—Everyday life.—Orphans.—The white princess.*
*PT2635.I65A256    1979      832'.9'12      78–20931*
*ISBN 0–8044–2714–3*

# TRANSLATORS' PREFACE

Any attempt at transferring literature from one language into another is of necessity a frustrating task. The experienced translator is all too well aware from the outset that his work will result in an ultimately imperfect rendition of the original text. In translating Rilke, the usual dilemma of literalness as opposed to "sense-within-a-greater-contextual-spectrum" becomes particularly difficult, largely because of the skillful manner in which young Rilke achieved a fusion of sense and sound within the framework of the German language.

A translation aimed at conveying the mood of the original work to the fullest possible extent sacrifices literalness; a strict literal translation is bound to violate the atmospheric nuances captured by the author, make idioms often appear incomprehensible, and, in the case of a play, all but preclude any possibility of stage production.

In working with the nine plays, the translators have sought to reproduce faithfully the spirit of the original texts while trying to adhere to Rilke's vocabulary, syntax, and sense of *milieu* as fully as their task would permit. Certain proper names (e.g., Georg, Helene, Frau Gärtner) were anglicized (George, Helen, Mrs. Gardner). In the very few instances where a character utters a phrase in French (perfectly common in terms of Rilke's *milieu*), the translation instead gives the corresponding English phrase. Excessively long German sentences were broken down into shorter English sentences—a measure confined almost exclusively to the stage directions.

The thorniest problem lay in the translation of Rilke's last complete play, *The White Princess*, written in rhymed verses, which marks the author's transcendence from "poetic drama" to "dramatic poem." It was decided to strive toward maintaining a feeling of the rhythmic quality of the lines without employing a rhyme scheme in the translation, rather than risk gross distortion of the ambiguity peculiar to the play's symbolism.

The translators are grateful to numerous friends and colleagues who gave freely of their time and counsel during the various stages of the translation process, especially to Professor Rochelle Wright and Mr. Christian-Albrecht Gollub in the Department of Germanic Languages and Literatures at the University of Illinois, Urbana-Champaign, to Rodney Farnsworth, to Debbie, and to the *Deep End* in Fayetteville, Arkansas, for encouraging the stage productions of *Air at High Altitude* and *The White Princess*.

*University of Illinois*                                                      K.P.

*University of Arkansas*                                                   J.L.

# CONTENTS

# INTRODUCTION

Rainer Maria Rilke (1875–1926), perhaps best known for his *Sonnets to Orpheus* and *Duino Elegies* and acclaimed as the century's foremost German-language poet, wrote more than twenty plays between 1894 and 1904. Since some of the plays no longer exist, the precise number is unknown. References to plays and plans for plays appear in letters and diary entries, but it is uncertain whether all the plays were in fact ever written.

This edition, comprising nine plays, contains the essence of Rilke's dramatic works. While the selection may appear arbitrary to a certain extent, the plays represented here include all those for which a performance has been documented, as well as those illustrating major developments in Rilke's dramatic ideology.

Rilke's earliest dramatic attempt was a three-act operetta libretto, *The End of the World (Der Weltuntergang)*, written during the summer of 1894 and destroyed in a fire. Later in the same year, Rilke turned toward the psychodrama: plays in which there is only one actor. Richard von Meerheimb, a popular writer of psychodramas during the late nineteenth century, became an example for young Rilke. Rilke's *Murillo*, based on the life of the Spanish painter, adheres to von Meerheimb's principles, although he clearly adapts these principles to his own purpose. For example, in contrast to the self-centered histrionics that characterize von Meerheimb's personages in a comparable situation, the death scene is dominated by an impassioned and yet restrained description of Christ upon the cross. Thus attention is shifted from the plight of Murillo's impending death to his attempt at rendering the passion of Christ. Other details of Murillo's death

appear to be Rilke's own invention. The biographical fact is that
the Spanish painter Bartolomé Estéban Murillo (1617–1682)
died in the arms of a patron, with one of his sons and a pupil also
present. But the play's primary significance does not lie in its
historical accuracy. The psychodrama kindled in Rilke the idea
of seeking to represent inner life versus outer experience, an idea
that was to remain with Rilke throughout all of his future works.

By the following year, 1895, Rilke had already begun to be
interested in the subject matter of naturalism, as is evident in
much of the poetry he wrote at that time. Virtually no modern
plays had been staged at Prague's two theaters prior to 1895,
when a major change occurred: suddenly works by Ibsen, Hauptmann, Rudolf Christoph Jenny, and others were performed. Rilke
was particularly taken with the pessimistic determinism of Jenny's
plays and decided to write such dramas himself. A year later,
Rilke's *"Now and in the Hour of Our Death . . ."* was staged in
Prague and translated into French for a potential performance
in Paris. The play contains a variety of standard naturalistic ele-
ments, but lacks the conciliatory tone so characteristic of Jenny's
plays. A family encounters difficulties due to illness, lack of
money, and villainy; the landlord will allow the family to stay if
the elder daughter consents to let him have his way with her. A
suggestion of Greek fate permeates the play as the sins of the
mother are passed on to the daughter. Yet this drama of seduction
and incest constitutes a curious fusion of naturalism and melo-
drama; it is filled with surprising revelations but ultimately is
overshadowed by a sense of inevitable doom.

The next play, *Early Frost*, appears to be a companion piece,
yet it stands in closer conformity with the postulates of naturalism.
In both plays, a family is threatened by economic demands, and,
although not figuring directly in these demands, the daughter is
persuaded by a villain that sexual submission is the only recourse.
In a traditionally naturalistic play, the protagonist is likely to
struggle against circumstances; Eva, in *Early Frost*, remains passive. She represents a higher consciousness trapped in a wicked
world, and is destroyed by this world, largely because of her
perceptions.

As far as sheer length is concerned, *Early Frost* is Rilke's most extended dramatic work. Principally as a result of his insistence on full presentation of background, motivation, and detail, Rilke was able to accomplish the creation of one of the most towering mother figures in modern German drama. Although essentially repulsive, Clementine is not a totally villainous character. She is steadfast in her beliefs and pursues her goal with indomitable perseverance. She is completely immersed in the material world and has come to terms with it. Since in her eyes her daughter has already become a whore, Clementine sees only one option: to protect her husband's secret and to preserve the home, regardless of the mental anguish this course may cause Eva.

Rilke later tempered the violent ending on Jenny's advice. The revised play deletes the final deaths. The present edition contains the original version, since it is free of outside influences and better illustrates Rilke's intent.

Symbolic undercurrents are already discernible in *Early Frost*, especially where Eva explains to Bauer the significance of "early frost." As Rilke's enthusiasm for naturalistic drama began to wane, he sought and found inspiration in the work of the Austrian playwright Ludwig Ganghofer, even writing a poem in his honor. Rilke was intrigued by the poetic quality of Ganghofer's latest play, but Ganghofer did not long remain the model he might have been.

Around June 1897, Rilke became deeply fascinated by the writings of the Belgian playwright Maurice Maeterlinck. In a series of essays entitled *Treasure of the Humble* (*Trésor des humbles*) Maeterlinck claimed that the domain of drama should be the inner processes of the soul and not the outer action of realism. Rilke found himself in agreement with many of Maeterlinck's tenets: outer silence must be maintained if the quiet, inner action of the soul is to be perceived, and thus it is necessary that good drama permit its actors to perform during lengthy pauses in speech; women are closer to the mystical truth of the soul, but all people possess an inner beauty and goodness; minor events are frequently sufficient to facilitate realization of the inner life; since our greatest events are inner actions that require no outer stimuli, the contemporary stage with its emphasis upon externals is an anachronism.

*Air at High Altitude*, Rilke's next play, heralds his transition from naturalistic to symbolistic drama. It was written shortly before Rilke became involved with Maeterlinck's theories and illustrates to what extent he had already formulated similar goals for himself. The personalities of Max and Anna are developed subtly and ironically. The cast of characters lists Max with his surname, Stark (which in German means "strong"), while his sister's name, Anna, stands alone. The play's title refers to the physical location of Anna's apartment as well as to her spiritual state. Upon the relative strengths of the two main characters is built a series of contrasts. Anna has found inner peace, while Max is an ex-officer and a lover without responsibilities and involvement in everyday realities: a soldier who has never fought and a lover who has never loved. Anna is engaged in life and can still know joy as she anticipates the opportunity to rejoin her parents and help her son; Max is bored, his laughter infused with cynicism. The symbolic mood pervades the action and succeeds in encompassing and suggesting all that Rilke intended. This mood is established in the harmonious conversations between Anna and the housekeeper and subsequently is tested in the conflict with Max.

The control of mood is also central to *Vigils*, an unconventional little play not so much because it leads the audience to a symbolic level (as does *Air at High Altitude*), but rather because of the oscillation between amusement and confusion that culminates in horror. Throughout the play, the stage is kept in almost total darkness. Only the outlines of certain objects, especially an armchair, are visible. There are many comic moments as the bumbling students and their girlfriends attempt to orient themselves— making this Rilke's only play to contain extended humor.

Details of the students' lives are irrelevant to Rilke's single purpose: to illustrate the experience of death in the midst of happy life. To that end, Rilke manipulates his audience: frequent pauses are used as a means of decelerating the action and giving the audience additional time to contemplate the developments— a device endorsed by Maeterlinck. From this play on, *"pause"* becomes a common item in Rilke's dramas.

The theme of *Not Present* is essentially similar to that of *Vigils*.

The play opens with an ordinary setting: a recently married girl is in the process of decorating her new home, assisted and counseled by her mother. Unlike *Vigils*, the element of horror is revealed gradually and unrelentingly. *Not Present* revolves around an erotic triangle composed of a married woman, her husband, and her sister. The sister never appears on stage. Her character is developed through the words of the husband, the wife, and the mother—a device that enhances the sister's mysteriousness. Even before the sister kills herself, slight shades of an almost supernatural quality pervade the play's mood. The spell seems broken when, in the final scene, Sophie and Ernst join forces against the phantom of the dead sister, strengthened by the impending birth of their child; but an element of doubt remains.

There are innumerable thematic resemblances between *Not Present* and Maurice Maeterlinck's *Aglavaine and Selysette*. Although there seem to be no references to this drama in Rilke's letters or diaries, it is certain that he was familiar with it. In his own play, Rilke seems to indicate his debt to Maeterlinck by giving the sister the unusual name Agla—an obvious hint at Maeterlinck's Aglavaine.

With *Not Present*, Rilke forsakes the theme of motherhood almost completely, even in his poems and stories. Scholars have argued that the shift to virginity and an outright rejection of the sexual act mirrors Rilke's actual state at the time. In leaving Prague in 1896, Rilke severed his ties with his mother and with Valerie von David-Rhonfeld, a girl with whom he had had a disappointing love affair. He never saw either of them again.

Similar in technique and theme to Gerhart Hauptmann's *Michael Kramer*, Rilke's *Everyday Life*, written in 1900, fuses lyrical intent with realistic form. According to the play's central theme, every experience has a certain rhythm in which it must be measured, and wisdom is the ability to find the rhythm for each individual situation. Instead of looking for moments of intense rapture in everything, one should find gentler rhythms for everyday experiences, rhythms that permit one to enjoy these everyday experiences to their limited fullness.

At the first performance in 1901, the audience did not like the play. Hugo von Hofmannsthal labeled Rilke's idea unsuitable for the theater. Since the play revolves around an idea, it makes considerable demands upon the audience. Despite Rilke's continued fondness for this work, there can be no doubt that he must have been extremely disappointed by the unfavorable reactions, and that these reactions were a considerable factor in his eventual decision to forsake any further attempts at drama. The play was performed several times after Rilke's death and appears to have been most successful in an adaptation for radio.

With his play *Orphans*, Rilke explores the psychology of children, juxtaposing their innocence and cruelty. Again reality stands in contrast with fantasy, as *Orphans* uncovers a dichotomous universe within the microcosm of the orphanage. The children's reaction to the death of little Betty is virtually void of emotion. Sympathy is replaced by curiosity and fear. Sensory impulses link the corpse with candles and cheese, since the children are unable to transcend the horizons of the material world. Jerome, the smallest boy in the group, is convinced that the little girl is not dead at all; he associates death with his mother's suicidal plunge from the top of a building. Because of this revelation, Jerome is ostracized from the group. As the old gardener removes the dead girl's coffin, Jerome pursues him. The play ends on an ambiguous note, similar to *Not Present*. It is not clear what will happen to Jerome; he may watch the gardener bury the little girl; he may or may not come to understand that she really has died; he may attempt suicide in order to join his mother. Ending the play in this fashion, Rilke forces the audience to enter the "theater of the mind."

Rilke's final attempt at drama resulted in *The White Princess*, his best-known play today. The idea for this play was formed during Rilke's stay in Viareggio in 1898, as he points out in a letter to Ellen Key:

> . . . *in Viareggio I had been deeply affected by the appearance of a begging black monk. I was standing at the window, and when he stepped into the garden, with his back toward the sea, a singular fear came over me that I must not move because, having noticed me, he would interpret any movement as a beckoning, as a call; and would come.* . . .

Rilke apparently felt that his apprehension was justified, because later that same day, his dog died under mysterious circumstances. A first version of the play was completed in 1899. It is more a lyrical poem than a drama and seems to illustrate Rilke's suggestion that drama and poetry should have a common aim. The substantially revised and expanded version reprinted in the present edition was written in 1904. One reason for its rewriting appears to have been Rilke's hope that the famous actress Eleonora Duse could be enticed to assume the title role. When Rilke met Duse years later, the offer made her momentarily enthusiastic, but the performance did not materialize.

There can be little doubt that Rilke wove into the character of the princess many features of a woman who by 1898 had already entered his life: Lou Andreas-Salomé. The princess's marriage of eleven years has been platonic; Lou's marriage, according to her own admission, was likewise platonic. In 1898, when the idea for *The White Princess* took form in Rilke's mind, Lou had been married for eleven years.

Despite the continued predominance of rhymed pentameter, the orchestral potential of language seems extended in the revised play; but it is rather that limitation of language that gives this play its character. As words become increasingly dull and useless tools, *The White Princess* culminates in total silence. The figures assume marionette-like qualities, embodying not only Maeterlinck's dogmas, but also those of Heinrich von Kleist, with whose works Rilke had by then become familiar. Thus, *The White Princess* completes Rilke's curiously circular path back to principles first stated in the psychodramas.

*Klaus Phillips*

# RILKE: Nine Plays

# Murillo

*A Psychodrama*

*Setting: A modest room of the unfamiliar house in front of which
the stranger was found unconscious.*

Oh! It—it hurts! I can hardly get up.
The seizure . . . What is this room? Where am I? . . .
Here . . . Nobody? . . . My memory was playing tricks,
my head feels heavy . . . and my veins are throbbing.
Oh, I'm tired . . . A heavy gray fog clouds
my eyes.—Steps?—Am I hearing right?—
A farmer? . . .

        Good friend, I can scarce remember
anything of the last few hours.
What happened? . . .

        Strange people found me
before your door? Motionless, rigid—as if dead?—

    (*Pause*)

Thanks! Your heart, which did not shun the stranger,
truly followed the Golden Rule.
. . . Yes, now I'm feeling wide-awake again:
I was out walking by myself.
Then, right on your doorstep, dizziness seized me . . .
In fear of my life, I caught hold of the doorjamb;
but then my arm fell, its strength gone, and my senses
        left me.
I don't know any more . . . But people, you say, found me
        thus? . . .

3

And you? You . . . give me your hand . . .

Thanks.

I feel dizzy again . . . Yes, I am very ill.
Who knows how soon my heart will stop its beating.

(*Pause*)

No, no, I know, good friend.
So send for a priest in a hurry,
one who provides the sick
the holy consolation of viaticum,
who easily can lead to light
transient thoughts
upon the bridge of wisdom's words.

(*Pause*)

What, am I hearing right? You have already done *that?*
And you have even found a doctor,
who is to come.—
My friend, it would be vain to think about recovery.
No! May only my sore soul get well now,
before it soars high upward,
filled with hope, into the realm of reward,
and there, before the steps of that heavenly throne
dissolves in splendor.

This is my longing . . . What?

The priest already?—Good, lead him to my bed!
But wait—it's getting hard for me to talk—
I have one more request.—Perhaps the last: Raise
the cushion for me . . . a bit . . . that's it—
and let me have a drop of water. How cooling it is!
There, thank you. You are pious and good.
You feel my pain with me and try to ease it gladly.
May God reward you and your children . . .
You do have some? . . .

(*Pause*)

See, how I guessed it.

That wrinkle, which shows around your lip,

that line of kindness led to my assumption.
I thank you once again.
                          Now, if you please,
let the dear, longed-for priest come in.
I am anxious to see him.

God be with you, your reverence. Enter.

You, friend, tell the ordained minister of God
of your good works, that with the sacred morsel
he may bless and give me strength for my last pilgrimage.
—Another thing—wait!
You took me in, friend, without knowing me.
Now you shall also know my name:
I am Murillo . . .

            (*Pause*)

I see you are astonished, almost incredulous,
and I read only doubts upon your face.
My garb, unadorned, without baubles and trinkets,
did not appear to you as worthy of the master?

            (*Pause*)

I have nothing with me but this iron,
a noble dagger, which once the prince presented me.
. . . You shake your heads? Look, I have nothing else
just now with which to prove my word.

            (*Pause*)

Nothing? And yet I do! It's in my hand,
the means with which to show you both the truth immediately.
Just move aside a bit . . . Acolyte!
Come forward, hand the incense burner to me.
The incense burner!—There . . .
I only take a little piece of coal.
Would you break it for me?
I am too weak . . . Fine. Big enough.
The sign upon the whitewashed wall shall speak for me:

(*Long pause*)

It shall be our Savior's head,
to serve as proof to you.
—As I long have been keeping it in my mind.
That anxious, plain-blanched countenance,
which speaks of agony and torture,
but also of divine submission . . .
*Thus* seems to me the messenger of true salvation.—
Bright—from his grief-veiled eyes breaks
a ray of love blessing us sinners . . .
Thus—is the glance of hope illuminated yet—
the pale lips seem to tremble slightly,
as if they voiced a sigh of unremembered pardons—
the breath of Spring of the redeemed world.—

(*Pause*)

Look here, friends! *Ecce homo*—see.
It is He! He drank the cup of bitter sorrow,
for us! . . .

         You raise your hands in prayer. . . .
You have understood my work.—

                I can die.

# "Now and in the Hour of Our Death…"

*A Play in One Act*

Characters:

MRS. GARDNER, *a widow*

HELEN ⎱ *Daughters of Mrs. Gardner*
TRUDY ⎰

LIPPOLD, *landlord*

THE SUPERINTENDENT

THE DOCTOR

*Time: the present. Setting: Mrs. Gardner's room. Mrs. Gardner is deathly ill: she is lying in the bed against the back wall. Helen, the elder daughter, about twenty-four, beautiful, blond, is busy at the stove. Then Trudy comes in—the younger daughter. She is thirteen years of age. Not beautiful, she has dark brown hair and somewhat too coarse features.*

MRS. GARDNER (*in bed, wrapped deep in blankets, groans in a feverish sleep*): Oh! Oh!

HELEN (*is warming broth in a brown clay bowl on the upper part of the stove. Anxiously*): Mother!

MRS. GARDNER *groans.*

HELEN: Oh God! (*She takes the bowl from the grate, lifts the lid.*) I'll wake her, the soup is warm. Mother! (*Softly approaches the bed.*)

TRUDY *comes from sewing class, a little basket on her arm. She skips in merrily, humming; then turns serious when she remembers her sick mother.*

HELEN: Shhh!

TRUDY *solemnly puts the basket away and on tiptoe comes nearer to the bed also.*

MRS. GARDNER: . . . He–len . . .

HELEN (*leans over her*): Yes, Mother?

MRS. GARDNER (*with effort*): It's—already—morning?

HELEN: It's noon, Mother . . . did you sleep well?

MRS. GARDNER: Noon . . . Noon . . .

HELEN: You fell asleep—around ten o'clock—do you remember, after the doctor had gone away.

MRS. GARDNER: The doctor? (*Quickly*) Yes, yes . . . now I remember.

HELEN: Now you'll have your soup, won't you?

MRS. GARDNER: Eat again already? . . . No, no . . .

HELEN: Yes, the doctor said you should; and when he comes back this afternoon . . .

MRS. GARDNER: Comes back? Today? . . .

HELEN: He just wants to have a look at you . . .

MRS. GARDNER (*gently*): Well, then give me the soup . . . (*Noticing Trudy*) Has Trudy had some yet?

TRUDY *shakes her head.*

MRS. GARDNER: No? Give—give . . . (*Her voice fails her; with motions of her hand, she tries to explain to Helen that she should give Trudy some soup first.*)

HELEN (*does as directed*): Yes, yes—there, Trudy! Now just keep still, Mother, or you'll get those cramps again.

MRS. GARDNER *leans back, groans.*

TRUDY (*pulls Helen by the dress, whispers*): Hey.

HELEN *turns to her.*

TRUDY: Listen, the teacher won't give me any money for your embroidery. It's over there in the basket. I brought it back: you know, it's better this way, keep it for yourself.

HELEN (*thinking*): . . . no money . . .

TRUDY: Factories do a better job and . . .

HELEN: No money . . . (*gets up*) and what about the other thing?

TRUDY: Oh, the job in the store . . . wait! She gave me a letter . . .

MRS. GARDNER *groans.*

HELEN: You'll have your soup in a second, Mother—coming!

MRS. GARDNER (*indistinctly*): Yes, yes . . .

*Trudy has gotten an envelope out of the basket; she hands it to Helen, who hurries to the window, quickly tears it open and scans the contents.*

HELEN (*shattered*): Nothing!

TRUDY (*spoons her soup, looking up*): My God, what's the matter? . . . are you getting sick, too, Hella?

HELEN: What will become of us?

TRUDY (*precociously*): *Again* they didn't take you in the store? —You should be glad. You won't have to stand behind the counter all day . . .

HELEN (*softly strokes her head*): Just eat, Trudy, your soup is getting cold.

TRUDY *turns away as if offended and quickly spoons down her soup.*

HELEN (*stands motionless a while; then pours part of the soup into a cup and sits down on the edge of the bed*): There, Mother, . . . there . . .

MRS. GARDNER: Soup?—

HELEN: Yes—Sit up a little bit. (*Helps her, arranges the pillow.*) Trudy, come help mother.

TRUDY (*helping childishly*): Feel better, Mother?

MRS. GARDNER *smiles weakly and kisses her softly on the forehead.*

HELEN: Here Mother, taste this. (*Gently and patiently raises spoon after spoon to her mother's lips.*)

TRUDY (*kneels by the bed*): Good, isn't it?

HELEN: Did you work hard at school today, Trudy?

TRUDY (*pouting a bit*): Of course; I've always been a good worker, haven't I, Mother?

MRS. GARDNER *shakes her head.*

HELEN: One more spoonful. To make you better.

TRUDY: Oh, yes, that's just what you always did to me when I was sick. And then one more for mother, and one for being good . . . (*Laughs.*)

MRS. GARDNER (*leans back, exhausted*): No—enough—enough.

HELEN: You've had so little!

TRUDY (*nestles up to Helen, feeling good toward her again*): And you, Hella, you haven't had anything at all to eat yet? . . .

HELEN: Oh . . . me!—

TRUDY (*takes the cup out of her hand*): Just wait! I'll give you some! There you go (*imitating Helen's voice*) one for mother . . .

HELEN *smiling, takes the spoon.*

TRUDY: And one for—for me!

HELEN: Little rascal!

MRS. GARDNER: Trudy!

HELEN: Trudy, mother's calling!

TRUDY: What is it?—

MRS. GARDNER: Do you have your book of fairy tales—here?

TRUDY: Fairy tales, of course. I know, I'll read to you again, Mother. (*Brings a chair to the bed, takes a book from the cabinet, and begins to read softly. Reads with childish intonation*): Then they came into a great and beautiful garden. In this garden were the most beautiful big flowers, and among the golden petals, in each flower, there sat little white live elves, blowing tiny flutes. And the sprightly springs danced to their beat and babbled so merrily that the two began to feel quite light and lively. And the prince said: "This is my garden. And someday all this will be yours, if only you stay true to me when I go out into the world to slay the big bad dragon, which has already killed so many innocent people." And the maiden blushed and said, "Oh, I will be true to you. Not because you are a handsome prince and because this golden castle and this beautiful garden with its living flowers belong to you, but because I love you with all my heart."

*Entirely absorbed in the story, Trudy pulls the chair closer to the bed and now reads more softly, so that only a whisper is heard. Helen has been standing the whole time in silence, her forehead pressed against the windowpane. Then the door opens a bit.*

THE SUPERINTENDENT: Miss!

HELEN: Oh, it's you! What . . .

THE SUPERINTENDENT: 'Scuse me, the landlord wants me to tell you that you should give me—really, I'm terribly sorry . . . that you should give me the . . . the money . . .

HELEN: Good heavens, dear Walker, tell him tomorrow, tomorrow morning . . .

THE SUPERINTENDENT: 'Scuse me, Miss, but . . .

HELEN: It can't be done, hard times, illness . . .

THE SUPERINTENDENT: Yes, but . . . he told me; 'scuse me, you know . . . I'm saying this just between us . . . if they don't pay, those people upstairs, he said, then they have to move out today . . .

HELEN: Today!

THE SUPERINTENDENT: Today, he said. Well, you wouldn't even put a dog out in the street . . . in this weather! I'm terribly sorry.

HELEN: Put in a good word for us, dear Walker. He thinks a lot of you.

THE SUPERINTENDENT (*perplexed*): Well . . .

HELEN (*to Trudy*): Keep on reading, Trudy . . .

THE SUPERINTENDENT: Then what should I tell Mr. Lippold?

HELEN (*desperately*): That we'll pay tomorrow, tomorrow morning . . . everything . . .

THE SUPERINTENDENT: Tomorrow then!

HELEN: Tomorrow . . .

THE SUPERINTENDENT: Well then, I'll tell him, I'll tell him.

HELEN: Go ahead, Walker, and put in a good word for us.

THE SUPERINTENDENT: Yes, Miss . . . yes . . .

MRS. GARDNER *groans.*

THE SUPERINTENDENT: Mrs. Gardner better?

HELEN *shrugs her shoulders.*

THE SUPERINTENDENT: It's a cross to bear! (*Wants to leave. In the doorway*) Right—nothing then . . .

HELEN: I told you already, tomorrow.

THE SUPERINTENDENT: Tomorrow. Well—then I was supposed to tell you, if you didn't pay anything, then I was supposed to tell you, that he'll come up here to see you, the landlord . . .

HELEN (*trembling*): Here!?

THE SUPERINTENDENT: Yes, I'm supposed to tell you. Right this afternoon . . . I'm terribly sorry, Miss . . . really sorry—well, good-bye.

HELEN *as if petrified, watches him leave.*

TRUDY (*sneaking up*): Hey—what's the matter?

HELEN (*absentmindedly*): Just read, Trudy, read.

TRUDY: But . . .

HELEN (*angrily*): Read!

TRUDY: Mother's asleep now.

HELEN: So what, you like to read out loud for yourself. Read out loud!

TRUDY *sneaks back to her chair.*

HELEN: Wait, Trudy, actually, actually you can get something for me. Get me, get me . . . yes, wait, mother is almost out of medicine (*picks up a little bottle*) there, you see, have them fill this for you at the pharmacy. There. And here's the prescription. There, go ahead, Trudy—get dressed. Hurry up!

TRUDY: I will! (*Surprised*) Does it have to be right now?

HELEN: Yes, right now . . . are you ready?

TRUDY (*while she puts on her jacket*): But what about money?

HELEN (*taken aback, frightened*): Money!? (*Calmer*) Yes, of course, for the medicine . . .

TRUDY: What did you think? Here's the prescription, it says on there how much it costs.

HELEN: Thirty Kreuzer . . . (*picks up her purse, counts*) ten, fifteen, twenty, one, two, three . . . (*softly*) my God, not even enough for *that*!

TRUDY: Alright, I'm ready . . . well?

HELEN: No, Trudy, it'd be better if you didn't go now, go later . . . in the evening.

TRUDY: You're fooling, aren't you?

HELEN: No, Trudy, stay with mother for now, stay in the room . . . when he, when he . . .

TRUDY: Well, I'm really beginning to wonder about you, Hella! . . . (*Goes to the back, puts her jacket away again, and comes up to Helen. Cajoling*) Don't be angry. Alright?

HELEN (*kisses her tenderly*): No, no, you're a good little sister; just sit over there and read, and when Mr. Lippold comes . . .

TRUDY: Lippold? *He's* coming to see us? that red-headed . . .
HELEN: Shhh! he'll be here, be good, Trudy, and read . . . Go
on now . . .
TRUDY (*unwillingly*): Alright, I'm *going.*

*Trudy goes back to her earlier spot on the edge of the bed and
picks up the book again; from time to time Mrs. Gardner is heard
groaning in her sleep; Trudy begins to read; as soon as Lippold
enters, her reading becomes softer and softer and she glances
furtively across the room. Finally she stops reading completely
and listens to the heated discussion with her eyes wide open.*

HELEN (*stands at the window. A knock at the door*): Come in!
LIPPOLD (*a small, short-necked, redheaded man with a well-kept
mustache; rather well dressed; features not unattractive but
brutalized; he approaches with a firm step, smiles, puts his
shining top hat on the cabinet*): Hello, hello, Miss Helen. Well,
Mrs. Gardner . . . feeling better? . . . feeling better? (*Without
waiting for an answer*) Hello, little one.
TRUDY *just nods, pouting.*
HELEN: Behave yourself! . . .
LIPPOLD: Oh, never mind . . .
HELEN: Please, Mr. Lippold, won't you sit down? (*Moves a chair
closer to the cabinet.*)
LIPPOLD (*sits down*): Thank you. Now down to business . . .
HELEN: Excuse me . . . read, Trudy.
LIPPOLD: I have come personally, dear Miss Gardner, to pick up
the money you wanted to pay today . . .
HELEN *turns pale, wants to speak* . . .
LIPPOLD: The trouble in Vienna, the bad times, everything so
expensive . . . in short, I need . . .
HELEN: Mr. Lippold, just *one* day!
LIPPOLD: Dear Miss Gardner, I'd like to, I'd like to . . . but
you've already put me off with that several times . . . and . . .
HELEN (*wringing her hands*): My God, just *this one more time.*
LIPPOLD: As I was saying: I'd like to, if I didn't need money my-
self this instant; in the thirty years I've been in business, things
have never been so bad . . .

HELEN: You see, my mother is so sick, so terribly sick.

TRUDY *pays attention.*

HELEN: Who knows whether . . . (*To Trudy*) Read, Trudy.

LIPPOLD: Well, I—that's really sad . . .

HELEN: And I'm doing everything I can. I'm working my fingers to the bone, and my eyes . . . red . . .

LIPPOLD: I know, you're—a hard worker . . .

HELEN (*overcome by a sudden idea*): You go to so many charitable events, Mr. Lippold. My embroidery, couldn't you? . . . (*She takes the little basket with her embroidery from the cabinet.*)

LIPPOLD (*smiling*): No, thank you, thank you—I'm up to my ears in stuff like that . . . (*Moving closer*) I can see already— we won't get anywhere this way.—Helen, haven't you understood the way I've been looking at you all this time . . . didn't it make you feel just a little bit hot . . . Didn't it . . .

HELEN *looks at him seriously.*

LIPPOLD: Really, Helen, I don't mean you any harm . . . Don't be afraid!—To make a long story short, I like you very much, Helen (*passionately*) . . . very much!

HELEN: Lord!

TRUDY: Mother's awake!

HELEN: Step back, for God's sake, Mr. Lippold, mother would be frightened if she saw a stranger here . . . there, back by the door, behind the stove, Mr. Lippold, there . . . thank you! (*At the bed*) Mother! . . .

MRS. GARDNER *moans loudly.*

TRUDY (*meanwhile, childishly*): Hey, what does he want?—

MRS. GARDNER: He–len . . .

HELEN: Do you want something? . . . a little water, maybe?

MRS. GARDNER (*tonelessly*): Water.

HELEN (*fills half a glass from the pitcher*): Here you are! (*She helps the old woman up; Mrs. Gardner sips from the glass and then sinks back again exhausted.*)

MRS. GARDNER (*tonelessly*): Wasn't . . . someone here? . . .

TRUDY: Mr. Lip . . .

HELEN (*puts her hand over Trudy's mouth; then softly*): No one, who would possibly . . .

MRS. GARDNER: . . . read . . . Trudy . . .

HELEN: Read!

MRS. GARDNER *groans, then becomes quieter again; she seems to fall asleep.*

TRUDY *reads so softly that only a whisper is heard.*

HELEN (*advancing toward Lippold*): The misery of it all! . . . the misery!

LIPPOLD (*coming nearer*): I want to help you. Your mother will have a nice place to stay down in my apartment and . . .

HELEN (*moved to joy*): You, you, Mr. Lippold!!!?

LIPPOLD (*coldly*): Certainly, if . . .

HELEN (*anxiously*): If?

LIPPOLD (*harshly*): If you will be mine . . . well? . . .

HELEN (*stumbles back a few steps and looks around the room gravely and hopelessly; then her glance falls on her sick mother . . . Suddenly and decisively*): Alright—I will marry you, Mr. . . .

LIPPOLD: . . . Marry?

HELEN *stares at him uncertainly.*

LIPPOLD: Marry, hm, that isn't quite what I said . . .

HELEN *completely horrified, understands his meaning. Her eyes are wide open, her whole body trembles, she supports herself convulsively on the cabinet.*

LIPPOLD *puts his hands in his pockets and looks at the floor in apparent ambivalence.*

TRUDY (*reads a little louder now*): And the prince put his arm around her and said: "Yes, you are good and pure like a flower, and your heart is as bright as a dewdrop. You deserve all the wealth I can give you. Yes, all my treasures are nothing compared to what your noble heart possesses, and the most beauteous sapphires of my crown are not so bright by far as your eyes . . ."

*Trudy looks around, surprised by Helen and Lippold's silence.*

HELEN (*tonelessly*): Just read, Trudy! (*To Lippold, icily*) Get out!

LIPPOLD (*with his hands still in his pocket, raises his eyes slyly*): Whaaat?—

HELEN: By God, get out!

LIPPOLD (*laughs shrilly*): Ha, ha, ha . . . You're showing me the
  door, you . . .
HELEN: Please! . . .
LIPPOLD: Who do you think *you* are? . . .
HELEN: I am not a—bad girl.
LIPPOLD: Bad! Poppycock! Bad!—Blessed be the innocent . . .
  simply ridiculous. You know, if a girl has something to gnaw
  on, then she can allow herself the luxury of such a virtue, just
  as some people keep a dog or a canary . . . but . . . you . . .
  And, by the way, they aren't bad because of *that*, not by a
  long shot. Lots of girls give themselves to men who don't even
  like them . . . and I . . . I! . . . (*passionately*) I! . . . (*Suddenly
  hoarse and theatening*) and then, if you don't want to, Missy—
  if . . . well! then . . . please—get your bags packed—there . . .
HELEN (*throws herself on her knees*): Have mercy on us!
LIPPOLD (*with growing passion*): If you think your mother will
  get well sooner and better in the street, if . . .
TRUDY *has put the book aside and stares wide-eyed at them. Mrs.
  Gardner groans.*
HELEN (*still kneeling*): Have mercy on us!
LIPPOLD (*beside himself, eyeing her beautiful body; his eyes
  burning with desire*): Helen! (*His voice is muffled, hoarse,
  feverish. Abruptly he jerks Helen to her feet and presses her
  body to his.*)
TRUDY (*however has jumped up, rushed toward them, and is
  hammering on Lippold's hands with her fists*): Hey you, what
  do you want with Helen . . . What . . .
LIPPOLD (*angrily lets go of the girl; he laughs shrilly to hide his
  anger*): Ha, ha, the brat! The little . . . get her out of here,
  Helen!
HELEN *shakes her head and presses Trudy's little head to herself.*
LIPPOLD (*takes his top hat from the cabinet*): Alright, Miss
  Gardner, you come to me at seven o'clock this evening, you
  will come to me . . . Helen? (*Threatening*)
HELEN (*horrified*): Never!
LIPPOLD (*still laughing*): Well, ha, ha, then everything is settled,
  Missy, then this place must be cleared out by seven tonight . . .
  Understood!? Ha, ha!

HELEN (*kneeling down again*): Please have mercy!

LIPPOLD (*smiling coldly*): One or the other; I keep my word. Think it over—Ha, ha, ha, ha. (*He puts on his top hat, takes another look around the room, and then goes out, whistling.*)

HELEN *leaning on Trudy for support, gets up and drops into the chair where Lippold had been sitting; she sobs violently; Trudy kneels by her.*

TRUDY (*strokes Helen's hair*): Now, now, you're not going to cry . . . because of him . . .

HELEN *sobs.*

TRUDY: Come on, stop it now; look! It's five-thirty already. The doctor will be here any minute.

HELEN: Five-thirty?

TRUDY: Of course, it's getting dark already.

HELEN (*dries her eyes*): God, what, what's going to happen to us!

TRUDY: Listen, Hella, I only had soup for lunch; I'm really hungry.

HELEN (*pulls herself together*): Poor Trudy. There's still bread left in the box, get some.

TRUDY *does as she is told, she finds a piece of bread in the cabinet and chews on it with her cheeks bulging; it keeps getting darker.*

HELEN (*still sitting*): See if there's a piece of candle left in the drawer.

TRUDY (*opens the drawer again*): Just a tiny piece.

HELEN: Let me have it.—Now we can have some light when the doctor comes. (*She gets up. Tired and broken, she goes to the table, lights the candle-stub, and places it on the tabletop.*)

MRS. GARDNER *groans.*

*Trudy walks back and forth, chewing on the breadcrust; Helen totters to he mother's bed and sits there without moving, her hands over her face. Only the ticking of the clock is heard. The candle flickers erratically. Scattered shadows chase through the attic room. Then a knock at the door.*

HELEN (*to herself*): The doctor.

TRUDY (*with her mouth full*): Come in.

DOCTOR (*rapidly*): Evening. Well?—(*To Helen*) Well, how's your mother?—She's been sleeping, hasn't she?

HELEN *nods.*

DOCTOR: Good, very good. But some light, my dear girl, light, I can't see anything this way.

HELEN: I'm sorry, we don't have . . .

DOCTOR (*annoyed*): Then at least bring me that candle. There. Hold it for me!

HELEN (*with the candle-stub at the bed*): Mother, the doctor is here.

MRS. GARDNER *mutters something incomprehensible.*

DOCTOR (*feels her pulse and shakes his head*): Fever, fever. (*Louder*) Are you in much pain, Mrs. Gardner?

HELEN: Are you in pain, Mother?

MRS. GARDNER (*faintly*): Pain? No . . .

DOCTOR (*stands up*): Well, everything's been done as I instructed; the medicine—You did have a refill made—didn't you?

HELEN (*at a loss*): I wanted to . . . if only . . .

DOCTOR (*abrupt*): Then why the devil do I even come here if you don't do as I prescribe! How do you expect . . .

HELEN: It's just that things are going (*hesitates, ashamed*)—so badly—for us now . . .

DOCTOR (*impatiently*): Well, that's very sad—but beyond treating your mother for free . . .

HELEN: But, Doctor . . .

DOCTOR (*without letting himself be interrupted*): I can do *nothing more.* You see, there are many like you . . . See that she gets her medicine. And strong soup, you understand, and a little wine; the old woman has lost all her strength.

HELEN: Is she better today, Doctor?

DOCTOR (*already leaving*): Better . . . better! When you don't even do as I tell you . . .

HELEN: Will you come again early tomorrow morning? . . .

DOCTOR: Tomorrow?! Well—there is a lot to do. By the way, my visit tomorrow will be—(*He interrupts himself abruptly.*) Well, we'll see. Don't forget the medicine! Good evening.

*He shuts the door behind him, then come back again.*

DOCTOR (*in the doorway*): Young lady!

HELEN *runs to him in fright.*

DOCTOR (*takes her hand; somewhat warmer*): Be prepared for anything. May God give you strength! (*Leaves.*)

HELEN (*screams*): My God!

MRS. GARDNER (*suddenly raises her head*): He–len! . . .

HELEN: Yes, Mother . . .

MRS. GARDNER: Cold . . . cold . . .

TRUDY (*who has been standing in the corner at the side of the mattress the entire time*): Of course, it's cold in here . . . I'll make a fire. (*She goes to the stove and begins to put in wood and make a fire.*)

HELEN *sits on the edge of the bed again.*

*An anxious silence falls upon them . . . the ticking of the clock is heard; Mrs. Gardner moans softly, now and then the firewood crackles softly, and sometimes Helen lets out a repressed sob.*

MRS. GARDNER (*begins to moan more and more intensely*): Helen . . . Helen . . . Something is strangling me—let in some air, air! . . .

HELEN: My God!

*Trudy sits motionless by the stove.*

MRS. GARDNER: God, Helen—hurry, hurry . . . (*Screams*) Air! *She raises her head up high; Helen takes her by the temples and kisses her perspiring forehead.*

MRS. GARDNER (*gradually becomes more quiet*): Air (*more softly*) Air (*more softly*) Air . . . *She sinks back, her throat rattling softly. Only from time to time does she groan softly. Helen holds her hand.*)

HELEN (*distraught, interrupted by sobbing*): Oh my God, my God, what should I do . . . help me just this once . . . don't let me despair now . . . I'm willing to sacrifice myself . . . I'll gladly sacrifice my life. But my virtue, God . . . God . . . surely . . . surely, this cannot be . . . Have mercy on me, I've been . . . good . . . God, God! (*She weeps*)

*Trudy sits in her chair; she has been watching her sister helplessly; now she is close to tears, too; she begins to sob. Silence again. There is a knock, no one moves. From the hallway a ray*

*of light falls into the room as the door opens. The superintendent
enters.*

THE SUPERINTENDENT (*softly*): Miss! Miss . . .

HELEN (*pale as a sheet, gets up softly*): Stand by me now, God.

TRUDY (*confidently skips up to the old man*): Oh, Mr. Walker!

THE SUPERINTENDENT: Psst! Miss Helen—'scuse me . . . but
everything's supposed to be out of here, everything . . . that's
what he said . . .

HELEN: Dear Mr. Walker!

TRUDY (*childishly*): What's supposed to be out?

THE SUPERINTENDENT: Well, 'scuse me—I really can't help it—
but it would cost me my job if . . . well, and I have children
and grandchildren . . .

*During these words it begins to strike seven. Voices are heard on
the stairs.*

THE SUPERINTENDENT: Here they come . . . to get your things . . .
well . . . (*Wants to go on in.*)

*A terrible struggle takes place within Helen; her expression re-
veals horrible agony. The tower clock strikes for the last time.*

HELEN (*rushes forward, highly agitated, grabs Walker by the
shoulder and whispers hoarsly*): Go to Mr. Lippold, quickly,
go and say . . . I . . . I'll come . . .

THE SUPERINTENDENT: What should I say?

HELEN: Tell Mr. Lippold that, that . . . I agree and—will come.

THE SUPERINTENDENT: I see-e-e.—

HELEN: But right away!

THE SUPERINTENDENT: Well—then—everything can stay here
. . . So, you agree and will come . . . come. (*Leaves.*)

*Helen rushes to her mother's bed, kisses her dangling hand
fervently.—Then she jumps up, pulls open a drawer from the
cabinet, ties her best scarf around her neck, and rushes to the
door. Speechless, Trudy has been watching her; now she grabs
her by the hand.*

TRUDY: Hella, what's the matter with you?

HELEN (*kisses her quickly*):—I'll be right back . . .

TRUDY: Don't go!

HELEN: I have to.

TRUDY: I'm afraid. The candle's going out.—

HELEN: Don't be silly, Trudy . . . I *have* to go now . . . (*In the doorway*) Trudy . . . sit down by mother; and if she calls for me, *don't* tell her I've gone.—

TRUDY (*anxiously*): No!

HELEN: Don't tell her, so she won't be frightened; I'm just going to get something . . . I'll be right back! So don't tell her.— (*Kisses her once more.*) God bless you!—(*Rushes out, steps are heard going hastily down the stairs, then a door opens, closes; then everything is still . . .*)

*Meanwhile the candle-stub on the table has gone out. The stage is in total darkness.—Trudy anxiously sneaks back to her chair by the bed. She sits down, everything remains completely quiet.*

MRS. GARDNER (*begins to groan more loudly again. She speaks feverishly*): No, no . . . I . . . can't . . . tell . . . her . . . no . . . Yes, I know it was . . . a big . . . big sin . . . (*moans*) . . . *big* sin . . . But . . . I was so young then . . . sin . . . No, not in the fire . . . it burns . . . Not . . . I repent . . . truly . . . (*A loud moan*) *Suddenly she wakes up; anxiously, but in a different,' wide-awake voice*) Helen! (*No answer*) Helen . . . are you there?—(*No answer*) (*Uneasy*) Helen . . . I'm better now— better—I can talk . . . I have to, Helen!

TRUDY (*softly and with hesitation*): Yes!?

MRS. GARDNER: There, Helen, give me your hand.—

TRUDY (*does so*): Yes.

MRS. GARDNER: There is still something on my heart. I have to tell you.—I know I'm going to die . . .

TRUDY *sobs.*

MRS. GARDNER: Don't cry!—Don't cry.

TRUDY: Mother . . .

MRS. GARDNER: Lord, Lord, just give me enough time . . . Now listen.—When I am dead, Hella . . .

TRUDY *sobs.*

MRS. GARDNER: When I am dead, go and take the packet of letters from the drawer there, and go with them to Lippold . . . he has to take care of you . . .

TRUDY (*astonished*): Lippold? . . .

MRS. GARDNER: He has to take care of you . . . *you*, Helen, it's

his duty! And he'll take care of Trudy also, out of charity.—
Listen . . . dear God, just enough time . . . Listen. (*Hastily*)
My late husband . . . Trudy's father, is not *your* father; before
I met him . . . I, I . . . forgive me . . . Hella . . .

TRUDY (*childish, not understanding*): Yes!

MRS. GARDNER (*with increasing haste*): Back then . . . I . . .
was very fond of Lippold, and he, he is your—father!

TRUDY *says nothing.*

MRS. GARDNER: Do you forgive me? (*Feverishly uneasy*) Give
me your hand . . . Do you forgive me?

TRUDY (*helpless and anxious*): Mother!

MRS. GARDNER: You see, it just happened that way . . . I know I
did wrong . . .

TRUDY (*helpless and terrified*): Mother!!!

MRS. GARDNER: You forgive me then . . . well, then go to
Lippold . . . when he sees the letters . . . he didn't recognize
me after all this time . . . but the letters . . . don't . . . forget
. . . there to the left . . . in the drawer . . . God . . . God! . . .
Now . . . now . . . (*Suddenly screaming*) Air, air! . . . Hel . . .

*A death rattle interrupts her. Piercing and dreadful it rises from
her chest; she jerks up one more time and sinks back with a shrill
cry—then everything remains completely still.*

TRUDY (*after a while*): Mother! (*Then again*) Mother! (*Finally
screaming*) Mother! (*Shakes the dead woman.*)

*Then the frightened child rushes to the door, flings it open so that
a broad stream of light penetrates inward; the distorted face
of the dead woman is now clearly visible among the shabby
pillows.*

TRUDY (*shouts fearfully down the stairway*): Hella! (*It echoes
resoundingly. Voices and the shutting of doors are heard.*)

TRUDY (*rushes back into the room, trembling. Anxiously, the
child looks around; then, as the voices come closer, she cowers
again on her chair and begins, trembling, with folded hands,
softly and with childish intonation*): Our Father, Who art in
heaven . . . hallowed be . . .

*Curtain*

# Early Frost

## A TWILIGHT PIECE

### A Play in Three Acts

*Characters:*

KLAUS GIRDING, *civil servant of the railway*
CLEMENTINE, *his wife*
EVA, *their daughter*
DR. FRIEDRICH BAUER
MERZEN, *businessman*
ANNA, *maid at the Girdings*
HANS, *son of Clementine and Girding, a high school student*

## ACT ONE

*Setting: a poorly furnished, middle-class room. Dull, dirty wall paint. The back door not quite in the middle. To the left of the same, a tasteless sofa covered in faded green rep fabric. Above it, family portraits in oval wooden frames. Against the left wall, a low cupboard; all sorts of worthless odds and ends on top of it. To the right, a writing table with crooked legs, shabby in appearance. Lying on it, Mrs. Clementine's hat and her bodice. In the foreground, the dining table with three cane chairs and an easy chair, in which Girding customarily sits. They are sitting at breakfast. Girding and his wife. Girding is reading the paper, she is keeping herself busy with the unmatched coffee cups.*

23

GIRDING (*in his easy chair. A shriveled-up, bashful creature with nervous eyes. He walks a little crookedly, has a drooping mustache, and a semicircle of curly hair that connects one ear with the other under his chin. Shivering, without looking up from the paper*): Hmmm. It's cold.

CLEMENTINE *heavy-set, with weak, blurred features. Her movements are sluggish and without grace. She occupies herself with the cups, without taking notice of Girding's remark.*

GIRDING (*louder, with emphasis*): It's cold, cold. I'll catch cold again.

CLEMENTINE (*still busy with the cups*): Nonsense!

GIRDING (*into the newspaper*): But you know the doctor told me . . .

CLEMENTINE (*surly, putting the cups aside and sitting down heavily*): The doctor! Does the doctor give you money for coal, too, hmm?

GIRDING (*lays the paper aside, stands up, creeps over to the sofa; picks up a blanket there; wraps it around his narrow shoulders. Then he sits back down in his easy chair. Sighs*): There.

CLEMENTINE (*looking at him contemptuously*): You're such an old woman! Oh, by the way, I'll tell you why you're always cold. How come you sat up here again last night writing?— You think they'll give you something extra if you make a slave out of yourself? You won't get a penny. They'll just laugh at you!

GIRDING (*mildly*): But . . .

CLEMENTINE (*keeps on talking*): They'll laugh at you, I'm telling you. Don't you see how they promoted the ones who were way behind you last year—hm!? Look at that Geschke, the old crook; he doesn't drag home the tiniest scrap of paper, and he even arrives late at the office all the time, as you keep telling me—and he, he's sitting way up in the administration now and playing the fine gentleman, and acting, Lord knows, as if he were the bellows pumper for some organ tune to which God sometimes gives the wrong pitch! . . .

GIRDING: Don't blaspheme, Clementine; I'll get up there too some day.

CLEMENTINE (*laughing, points her finger at him*): You!

GIRDING (*with forced composure*): Yes, I.

CLEMENTINE: Maybe after the dirty truth about the three hundred guilders gets out?

GIRDING (*terrified*): Clementine!?—

CLEMENTINE: Well, it's the truth. When it happened you said: nobody'll find out, we have to do it, for the children, for Eva . . . for Hans . . .

GIRDING (*trembling*): But didn't you get a vacation in the country? . . .

CLEMENTINE: Of course! You sent us out into the middle of nowhere—for a vacation.

GIRDING: But Eva got better, after all.

CLEMENTINE: Yes, she came back burned to a crisp. Then you let us starve twice as much and . . . Certainly. We didn't see much of the three hundred guilders. You went through the rest right here . . .

GIRDING (*wants to speak*): . . .

CLEMENTINE: Just be quiet. Didn't you tell us you were in the tavern every night?

GIRDING: But that drop of beer . . .

CLEMENTINE: You can't do without that. Even if your wife and children go to the dogs.—Your drop of beer . . . Where else would the money have gone? (*Slowly and with emphasis*) Three hundred guilders. And you think Eva and I used them out there in that Godforsaken place? You know what we ate for dinner? Bread, dry bread . . . And just take a look at Eva now, how weak and thin and pale she is again. And the clothes she runs around in! She's had that same winter coat for five years. Five years! She looks like a beggar.—People might start giving her spare change. You ought to be ashamed.—I won't even talk about myself; it wouldn't do any good. You have to have your—drop of beer!—

GIRDING (*firmly and then more and more timidly*): No, Clementine, you can't put the blame on me. Whatever I kept back (*hesitates*) . . . kept back from the till . . . the till at the railroad—is on your conscience. I never would have done it! Lord knows! I'm much too honest.

CLEMENTINE (*jumping up*): You spineless coward! You shove it off on me, on me? ...

GIRDING (*collapsed, murmurs*): No, I was honest.

CLEMENTINE: I don't give a damn about your honesty! You understand? You and your honesty! For its sake your wife and daughter can starve to death.—Nobody ever got fat on honesty! —But it's not my fault what you did. You can forget that.— I told you then: do what you want ... (*The door bell rings. Mrs. Girding goes to the door and keeps repeating irritably*) Do what you want, do what you want ... (*She exits through the center door in order to answer.*)

GIRDING (*sits motionlessly and stares off into space. His mouth is gaping slightly. A lethargic stupor is reflected in his eyes. He mumbles while stroking his forehead with a shaking hand*) God forgive me my sins ...

*Clementine comes back, a letter in her hand.*

GIRDING (*his hand still covering his eyes*): Who was it?

CLEMENTINE: Here. (*Holds the letter out to him.*) Here! (*Throws it on his lap.*)

GIRDING *after holding it up to the light, opens it carefully with the coffee spoon.*

CLEMENTINE (*meanwhile touches the coffee pot*): Naturally it's all cold. What's keeping Eva this time? All of a sudden she gets used to sleeping late. (*Viciously*) The princess. (*Goes to the door at the right. Calls*) Eva! (*Even louder while she knocks*) Eva!

EVA (*from within*): Yes!?

CLEMENTINE: Hurry up now. It's getting cold. You hear?

EVA: Yes!

GIRDING (*meanwhile reads the letter with growing terror. Suddenly he drops it and sighs*): Holy Mother of God!

CLEMENTINE (*casually*): Hm!?

GIRDING (*tonelessly*): ... from Merzen.

CLEMENTINE: So what?

GIRDING (*very weakly*): He wants his money.

CLEMENTINE (*with impertinent indifference*): And ... and ... ?

GIRDING: And what—I don't have any ...

CLEMENTINE: So don't give him any, what can Merzen do to you?
GIRDING (*trembling*): What can he do to me? He can make me lose my job, my name, everything.—
CLEMENTINE: Merzen?
GIRDING: He knows . . .
CLEMENTINE: He knows . . .
GIRDING: About my, my . . . indiscretion.
CLEMENTINE: Bravo—that was really clever.—Trusting a crook like that. You're an idiot.—
GIRDING: What, what now? (*Perplexed, shattered*)
CLEMENTINE: Now you're in for it. Serves you right.
GIRDING (*perplexed*): My God!—
CLEMENTINE: You really are a miserable old woman. Shame on you! Do I have to do all your thinking for you? I have an idea.—
GIRDING *looks at her in disbelief.*
CLEMENTINE (*rudely*): Well, don't just sit there with your mouth open!
GIRDING: You have any money?
CLEMENTINE: No.
GIRDING: Then how can you? . . .
CLEMENTINE (*softly*): Eva will have to pay . . .
GIRDING (*in great astonishment*): What?!
CLEMENTINE: Are you deaf? Eva will have to pay, I said . . .
GIRDING (*more astonished*): Eva!?
CLEMENTINE (*sits down*): Didn't you ever notice how Merzen acted toward her every time he was here?
GIRDING: No.
CLEMENTINE: You're really a fool. A blind man would have seen it! All day long he was after her, with "Miss Eva" here and "Miss Eva" there . . .
GIRDING: And what do you want? . . .
CLEMENTINE: What do I want? You still don't know?—
GIRDING: Well, tell me . . .
CLEMENTINE (*with brutal calm*): He'll get her instead of the money! That little thing is still worth something!—
GIRDING: But Clementine, don't joke. Eva is as good as engaged to Bauer . . .

CLEMENTINE (*scornfully*): As good as—engaged! I know all about that! As bad as—in love with the girl, he probably was, this nobody.—As good as—engaged! Oh, good heavens. You said the same thing four years ago when that other scoundrel ran off with the little seventeen-year-old. And then you saw what happened: good-bye! And we didn't get one penny— and all the shame on top of it!—And now it's going to start all over again. The business with "the doctor." He's a really fine gentleman . . .

GIRDING: Eva likes him.

CLEMENTINE: Likes, likes!—Don't talk so big. A girl like her likes anyone who acts a little sweet and nice to her. My God! She doesn't have to tie herself down to one man yet!—And Bauer, I'll knock him out of her skull. He'll leave her anyway— you'll see . . .

GIRDING: Dr. Bauer is an honest . . .

CLEMENTINE: You know what you can do with your "honest," I've heard it before!

GIRDING: So you think Eva should marry Merzen?

CLEMENTINE (*shamelessly*): Marry or not! He shall *have* her!

GIRDING (*flaring up*): Woman!

CLEMENTINE: Now, now, now, now, you worthless moralizer, not so fast!—Maybe you'd rather be thrown in jail.

GIRDING (*shaking*):   . . . I . . . I . . .

CLEMENTINE: Just let me handle it. We'll take care of Merzen! If he marries her, well and good; and if he throws her over afterwards—we'll really have him in the palm of our hand. Yes, I'll see to that! If you had a brain like mine, Girding, you would have been general manager long ago, I'll tell you that . . .

GIRDING: But how will the poor child . . .

CLEMENTINE: Leave that up to me! And now, be quiet. I hear her coming.—Isn't it time for you to go to the office?—

GIRDING (*looks at the clock*): Eight thirty. In a minute, in a minute . . . (*Sinks back down, wrapped deep in the shawl.*)

MRS. GIRDING *pours the cold coffee into a cup and puts it down at the empty place to the left.*

EVA *enters. A pale, blond girl with beautiful but somewhat care-worn features, an expression of sadness in her large eyes. She moves rather stiffly and awkwardly. Her hair is parted in such a way that the extreme tips of her earlobes are covered. She goes over to her father. He rises. She bends over and he kisses her on the forehead.*

EVA: Morning, morning, Papa.

GIRDING: Good morning, my child.

EVA: Did you have a good rest, Papa?

CLEMENTINE (*interrupts*): Well, it seems to me that *you're* the one who had a "good rest." Just look. Eight thirty.—

EVA: I was so tired, Mother!

CLEMENTINE: Tired, young lady. You don't say. From lazing around all day.—

EVA: I don't laze around, Mother!

CLEMENTINE: No, you read all day and . . .

EVA: And don't I do everything in the kitchen? . . .

CLEMENTINE: That little bit of food cooks itself.

EVA: You don't want me to go and learn to teach kindergarten.

CLEMENTINE: You want to be some kind of hired girl, do you, Princess?

EVA: Why not, if I can earn some money for myself . . .

CLEMENTINE: That would be the right thing for you! No, I won't let you be a hired girl! That would really shame us in the eyes of everyone.

GIRDING: There is no shame in work.

EVA: Right, Papa, that's what I say, too.

CLEMENTINE: Don't bother me with all this old, worn-out poppy-cock that no one believes in anymore! Don't make me laugh! It's no shame! But it's no fun either. And it would be a sad cross to bear if a girl like you, Eva, couldn't find a better way to earn her money.

EVA (*astonished*): A better way!?

GIRDING: I have to go to the office. What's it like outside, child?—

EVA (*goes to the window*): Rather dismal and stormy. The way it is in the fall—in the fall . . .

*She comes back from the window shuffling her feet, and while her mother clears the table in front on the left side, she helps her father put on his overcoat.*

EVA: There, Father, put your collar up. It's still early.

GIRDING: Thanks, thank you, Eva dear.

EVA (*with the umbrella*): And here's your umbrella.

GIRDING: Thanks.

EVA: (*with his hat*): Your hat.

GIRDING: There!—Well, I'll be going now.—Well . . .

CLEMENTINE (*impatiently*): You'll be late again!—

GIRDING: I'm on my way.—Yes.—And what I wanted to say . . .

CLEMENTINE: Save it till this evening.

GIRDING: Alright, alright . . . (*Moves slowly and hesitatingly, Eva behind him. At the door he turns and kisses the girl tenderly on the forehead.*)

GIRDING: God bless you! God bless you! You poor child! (*Exits.*)

EVA (*startled*): What did Papa mean by that?

CLEMENTINE: Nothing. (*Harshly*) You know he's not himself sometimes . . . But wait, now we have to clean up here. Just look at the cupboard. It hasn't been dusted for a week. And the desk is all messy too.—Come on, help me.

EVA: Alright, let me have a rag.

CLEMENTINE (*throws one to her*): There.

EVA *drops it.*

CLEMENTINE: You certainly are clumsy.

EVA (*bends down*): Oh!

CLEMENTINE: Now it even bothers you to bend over?

EVA: I'm just tired.

CLEMENTINE: Go on, go on, I'll put some life back into you. We have a guest coming.

EVA (*astonished*): A guest?

CLEMENTINE: There, you see, it's a surprise! Well? Guess who it is. A gentleman, of course, a fine gentleman.

EVA: I wouldn't know. Surely you're joking, Mother.

CLEMENTINE: Not in the least.—You'll see! And now let's get the room ready for him.

EVA: *This* room?

CLEMENTINE: I'll have my bed brought in, and I'll take that thing there for the time being (*pointing at the sofa*).

EVA (*more astonished*): Your bed?—

CLEMENTINE: Don't act so surprised. We can't just have a guest come and bed him down on that old flattened-out sofa. His guts would get all twisted up if he had to sleep there.—And if we care at all about the guest . . .

EVA: Who is it, Mother?—

CLEMENTINE: Aha, now you're curious. A handsome gentleman, my pet, a fine gentleman whom your papa holds in high esteem, and to whom you must be very sweet, very, very sweet.—

EVA: Be very sweet to him. (*Lowers the rag.*)

CLEMENTINE: Of course!—I'm telling you! He's coming today; he may be here in an hour. Mr. Merzen.

EVA (*disappointed, goes back to her dusting*): Oh—him!—

CLEMENTINE: Him, well, who else? Just don't go around belittling everything in the world—you stuck-up little thing, you! Who do you think you're waiting for? Another nobody who'll run off with you, hmm?—

EVA: Mother!

CLEMENTINE: Well, it's the truth! Do you think it's a special privilege for anyone to catch a girl who's already gone through a dirty love affair . . .

EVA *breaks out into loud sobs.*

CLEMENTINE: No crying! That's no help at all. Don't blame yourself. The flesh is weak. I just mean to tell you: don't play hard to get. You understand? You have to grab with your hands and feet if someone comes along. And Merzen certainly wouldn't be so bad.

EVA *raises her hands from her tearful eyes and looks at her mother in mute horror.*

CLEMENTINE (*who is afraid she may have said too much for the present, anxiously*): Don't look at me that way. It's just a thought. I only meant . . . Or maybe you still have that silly doctor on the brain?

EVA: Friedrich has always been sweet to me, Mother!

CLEMENTINE: Always sweet, poppycock!

EVA: I won't stand for any criticism of him . . .

CLEMENTINE: Fine, fine! You defend your doctor. If he comes to get you—it's alright with me—I have nothing against it!

Nothing at all. But why doesn't he ever show his face around here? He hasn't been by to see us for over six months.—

EVA (*drops into a chair. Tonelessly*): He has to work.

CLEMENTINE (*blinking her eyes*): Hmmm? Work! So what.— No, child, don't keep your hopes up for him; he has other ideas, that doctor. Today or tomorrow he'll marry a rich girl, and then you'll be jilted for the second time and crying your "Oh's" and "Dear me's" all over the house again.—But then I won't have any sympathy for you . . . Well, the cupboard's done. Now the room looks a little better. Dust the desk—Eva.

EVA: I'm not doing anything for him. (*Remains seated.*)

CLEMENTINE: For whom?

EVA: For Merzen!

CLEMENTINE: Silly thing! (*Goes and tidies up the desk herself.*) What's the time? (*Eagerly polishes the soiled tabletop.*)

EVA *still sits in the same spot and stares at the floor.*

CLEMENTINE (*looks at the clock herself*): For goodness sake— eleven! Hans will be coming home from school any minute. Anna's not here yet either. I'll have to make the fire myself again. How miserable!

EVA *sighs.*

CLEMENTINE: Oh, you're really suffering!

*The door bursts open. In runs Hans, a sixteen-year-old high school student in the prime of high-spirited youth. His winter coat is open. His cheeks red. He throws his books on the nearest chair.*

HANS: Hello, Mother! Damned windy today. Really takes the breath away.—Hello, sister! How are you?—You're sitting there again like a lamb ready for the slaughter. Ha, ha, ha, ha. —Something's got you upset again.—(*Goes up to her, bends down to look into her face—then with pathos*) How can you tolerate it, Mother? All the time this miserable sourpuss from morning till night.—It's really disgusting!—

CLEMENTINE (*meanwhile walks up and down in the room from the cupboard, to the desk, to the sofa. Nods approvingly*): There.

HANS: Tell me, Mama, are you expecting Prince Charming here today? Certainly looks damn clean here. Hm, the cupboard. I've been throwing all my old trash there for weeks—but it's all cleaned off today. (*With an impudent look, referring to Eva*) Is by any chance a suitor coming for her there? . . .

CLEMENTINE: Mr. Merzen's coming.

HANS: Merzen! Hurray, that'll be dandy! He'll bring some life back into this boring damned place. He knows how to tell a story. You know, Mother, things you can't repeat. But they've really happened to him, heh . . . heh . . . Hey, by the way, this works out perfectly. Professor Schwab's sick. You know Schwab, the one with the big red nose who goes around all the time without a tie and has the pretty daughter.—He's not coming today, so we're off.—And if Merzen comes, he'll take me out to the cafe. It'll be some afternoon!—

CLEMENTINE *about to leave the room.*

HANS: Mama, by the way—I've got some news! And you there, Miss Mopey, ha, ha, ha, this'll interest you. A friend of mine told me.—The blond "doctor," you know, that "learned" jackass who always used to come here, and always kissed Eva's hand . . . (*He imitates.*) My dear girl . . . (*He bows, acts as if someone has given him her hand, kisses the air with repulsive affection.*) My dear girl, I kiss your hand . . . I . . .

EVA (*jumps up*): What's happened to him?—

HANS: Oho—little sister's getting wild—now I won't tell! (*He crosses his hands behind his back and walks backwards whistling.*)

EVA (*rushes after him*): Tell me, Hans, tell me.

HANS *keeps on whistling.*

CLEMENTINE: Oh, go on and tell her.

HANS: Wait, Mother, I'll whisper it in your ear. Come here. *Mrs. Girding leans over to him. He whispers something in her ear, visibly amused. Eva stands off to the side, trembling.*

CLEMENTINE (*looks knowingly*): Ohhhh!

HANS (*aloud*): Yes, and in a week they'll have the wedding!

EVA *lets out a soft cry and rushes out through the center door.*

HANS: Ha, ha, now I've given it away after all. That really got her.

CLEMENTINE: I'll go and make the fire now.

HANS: Mama, you know something: I'm hungry as a bear. Bring me some bread and butter.

CLEMENTINE: You can't have any butter.

HANS: Alright, then bread! Bread! I don't care!

CLEMENTINE (*opens the upper drawer of the cupboard, takes out a loaf of bread and cuts a hefty piece*): This alright?

HANS: Well, yes, if it won't get any bigger. (*Takes a big bite.*)

*Mrs. Girding leaves. He walks up and down the room, quickly biting off chunks, his left hand in his pants pocket and the piece of bread in his right. Then he hums a popular tune.*

EVA (*comes in through the door on the right. She is very pale and her steps seem uncertain*): Hans!

HANS (*turning around*): Well?

EVA: Tell me who told you all this.

HANS (*harshly*): What?

EVA: What you said before.

HANS (*raises his eyebrows*): That worries you, doesn't it, sis?

EVA: Tell me.

HANS: No.

EVA: You're such a stubborn little schoolboy!

HANS: I'm whaat?

EVA: A disgusting, stupid brat!

HANS (*flaring up*): Listen!

EVA: No, oh please, Hans, tell me!

HANS: I don't want anything from you—I don't need anything from such an—old crow!

EVA: Wouldn't you like to have an herbarium?

HANS: Of course.

EVA: I'll buy you one.

HANS: Don't try to fool me now.

EVA: I promise, I'll buy you one.

HANS: Really?

EVA: That's what I said.

HANS: Let's shake on it. The right hand, there.

EVA: And now you'll tell me . . .

HANS: Alright. Dr. Bauer's nephew, the little redhead, he told me.

EVA: He knows for certain?

HANS: Why wouldn't he know if his uncle's getting married?

EVA: And who is he marrying?

HANS: Who? Hm! She's supposed to be rich, very rich.

EVA: But who? Who is she?

HANS: (*turns around, surprised*): Boy, what *don't* you want to know about all this? (*Curtly and slyly*) That I don't know.

EVA: Hans! (*Imploring*)

HANS (*angrily*): But I don't know, on my honor I don't! (*Goes to the cupboard, takes out a few odds and ends from there, examining them in his hand and whistling.*)

EVA (*embarrassed, moves to the front. She takes something out of her pocket. Hesitatingly*): Hans, dear.

HANS (*stopping. Drawn out*): Hmm?

EVA: Would you like to do something for me?

HANS: Depends.

EVA: You know you're going to get the herbarium.

HANS: That's understood.

EVA: Well, would you do me a favor?

HANS: Do I get the big, wide one with the red top?

EVA: That's the one.

HANS: Well, what is it?

EVA: Do you know where Dr. Bauer lives?

HANS: Where he lives. Hm. Wait a second. Dr. Bauer . . . (*Thinking*) I know: Quergasse 110.

EVA: Would you go there and take a letter to the porter?

HANS (*puts his hands behind his back and leans forward*): A letter?!

EVA: Yes, I think it would be quicker and safer than by mail.

HANS (*without changing position*): A letter from *you*!?

EVA (*softly*): Yes.

HANS *turns around on his left heel like a top and lets out a long whistle.*

EVA (*looks embarrassed*): Will you? . . .

HANS (*threatening with his finger*): It seems to me, it seems to me!

EVA: Please, Hans!

HANS: It's alright with me; I don't care. Give it here.

EVA: You promise that you'll give it to him.

HANS: I promise. Let me have it. (*She gives him the letter.*)

EVA: And right away.

HANS: Right away. And you, don't forget the herbarium.

EVA: Yes, yes, the red one. Can I depend on you?

HANS: Yes, I think so, since I gave you my word! (*Proudly, as he puts his hand between the second and third buttons of his jacket*)

EVA (*moves slowly again toward the door on the right. There she turns once more*): And see that they take it up to him right away.

HANS (*bows roguishly*): This very instant, at your command.

EVA *exits.*

HANS (*puts on his winter coat with exaggerated movements, puts on his hat—smirks. He stops again at the door, takes out the letter and reads*): To Dr. Friedrich Bauer—ha, ha, ha, little sister—there is something—behind all this.—If I told mama, that would be something!—But no, I'm getting that herbarium out of it. (*Holds the letter up to the light as if to read it. Then resolutely puts it in his pocket.*) Well, it's alright with me!— (*As he touches the doorknob, Clementine's voice is heard outside.*)

CLEMENTINE: Please, won't you come right in. Of course! Got your lovely letter! Yes; we've been looking forward to this. Yes, especially Girding, especially him.—Please—please—just walk right in— right in here!

MERZEN *enters; a tall figure. Flat forehead, restless eyes. Straight hair combed forward. Dressed with uncoordinated elegance. A small travelling bag in his left hand. He speaks rather quickly with a disagreeable, affected intonation.*

*As Hans hears the voices, he steps sideways from the door and pulls off his hat. Merzen walks straight through the room without observing Hans. Hans makes a few stiff bows without being noticed. Clementine comes in behind Merzen, talking incessantly.*

CLEMENTINE: No, it's really nice of you to have thought of us again, really very nice!—Girding, he was always saying: My, Merzen hasn't been here in a long time.—My, where could

Merzen be keeping himself.—You'll have to pardon me, he always calls you Merzen, Mr. Merzen.

MERZEN *smiles with a superior air.*

CLEMENTINE: Now just put your bag down over there, and your hat, and sit down and make yourself comfortable. (*Pushing a chair forward*) There, sit down, please.

MERZEN (*sits down*): Thank you, thank you, Mrs. Girding . . . tell me . . .

*Clementine sits down. Hans is still standing in the back.*

CLEMENTINE (*without listening*): You don't look too well, Mr. Merzen.

MERZEN (*affectedly*): Well, this constant travelling, this constant travelling, today here, tomorrow there, and even when one travels in comfort . . .

CLEMENTINE: Oh, yes, of course!—And those uncomfortable, strange beds and the restaurant food . . .

MERZEN: Yes indeed.

CLEMENTINE: You must have come a long way this time.

MERZEN (*looking up*): I just came from Vienna.

CLEMENTINE: Vienna, I know it well.

HANS (*takes a few steps forward*): But Mama, you told me . . .

CLEMENTINE and MERZEN *look around in surprise.*

CLEMENTINE (*behind Merzen's back*): Psst! Psst! (*Aloud*) Oh, Mr. Merzen, please excuse my son Hans.

HANS: Yes, yes. (*Bows.*)

MERZEN (*jovially, condescendingly*): We've already met, haven't we, young man . . .

HANS: Oh, yessir.

MERZEN (*offers him his hand*): You've grown, too! Going to high school, are you?

HANS: Yes.

MERZEN: Latin, Greek, well, how are they coming along?

HANS: So so . . .

MERZEN: Well,—it's one of those things.

CLEMENTINE: I always say, these poor children have to study so much. It's really awful. And I ask you, what do they need all that rubbish for anyway. Will it do them any good in life? Did you ever need it? You went to high school, too, I'm sure.

MERZEN: I? hm (*clears his throat*) well—that is . . . well, how is Girding getting along?

CLEMENTINE: Thank you for asking. So so; it seems like he needs the whole pharmacy most of the time. My, I'm telling you, Mr. Merzen, he's always got a pain here and a pain there —the way the money keeps pouring into the doctor's pockets—

MERZEN: I see . . .

CLEMENTINE: And he always wants it warm in the room—I don't know anymore where I'm supposed to get the coal. In the fall now, when other people haven't even started to heat their houses . . .

MERZEN (*who has been watching first Clementine and then Hans, who is standing there with his hands in his pockets; abruptly*): But you look very well, dear Mrs. Girding, and the . . . the young man too—hm—really as if he had a good tan—very well indeed.

HANS: Yes, just think, it was a great summer, we were in the country . . . in . . .

CLEMENTINE *glares at him, he bites his lip and breaks off, frightened.*

MERZEN (*drawn out*): Ohhhh?!

CLEMENTINE: All he means is—well, that is—(*winking continuously at Hans*)—that is . . . we were invited out there for a few days . . .

MERZEN: I see.—

HANS (*coming forward*): I'm going now, Mr. Merzen. Good-bye. —I have to . . .

MERZEN: Alright, good-bye!—He really looks terrific.

HANS *exits quickly through the middle door.*

MERZEN (*to Clementine*): Yes, your children must make you very happy.—I'm glad you were in the country . . .

CLEMENTINE (*embarrassed*): Invited.

MERZEN: Invited—yes. It's always nice when you can afford it.— You certainly have to keep something squirreled away (*with emphasis, looking sharply at Clementine*) you know, even when you're invited; the trip and all that, it adds up . . . but it's always nice when you can afford things like that . . .

CLEMENTINE (*wants to say something, but doesn't find the right words, and contents herself with a laugh. Finally she stammers out the words with difficulty*): May I offer you a glass of wine?

MERZEN (*curtly*): No, thank you.

CLEMENTINE: Well, it's almost time for dinner.

MERZEN *looks at his watch.*

CLEMENTINE: Won't you give us the pleasure of having a little soup with us?

MERZEN: Sorry, I have an appointment with some colleagues.

CLEMENTINE: Oh, that's too bad.—But I can't let you go, dear Mr. Merzen. Girding would never forgive me!

MERZEN: But . . .

CLEMENTINE: No excuses now—please! Of course you can't expect anything fancy. Just plain, simple, home-cooked food . . . the way it is with poor people . . .

MERZEN *looks sharply into her eyes during these last words.*

CLEMENTINE (*parrying*): Servants are such a burden, you can't depend on any of them. Our maid—we can't afford one who sleeps in—is always late . . . and so you'll have to be satisfied with whatever my daughter . . .

MERZEN (*looking up*): Your daughter?

CLEMENTINE: Yes, Eva, you know . . .

MERZEN (*affectedly*): Oh, Miss Eva, how could I ever forget, Heh, heh, heh . . . How is she?

CLEMENTINE (*shouts*): Eva!—Well, so-so—doesn't quite want to come out of her shell, that girl.

MERZEN (*sharply*): In spite of the vacation in the country?

CLEMENTINE (*clearing her throat*): Yes.—What I wanted to say, so I won't forget—You'll stay overnight with us this time, won't you, Mr. Merzen?

MERZEN: What?!

CLEMENTINE: Well, I mean, it would be a lot more comfortable, I have these good beds that I inherited from my grandmother . . .

MERZEN: But I couldn't possibly . . .

CLEMENTINE: Oh, why not, I can put a bed in here for you—a blanket or quilt, whatever you prefer, and a basin over there on the cupboard . . . If that's not too modest for you . . . (*Shouts again*) Eva!

EVA (*inside*): Coming!

MERZEN: I really don't know, Mrs. Girding—no, I absolutely cannot accept, under no circumstances . . .

CLEMENTINE: But . . .

EVA (*in the doorway*): What is it? (*Notices Merzen and wants to go back; then she makes up her mind and walks slowly to the front . . .*)

MERZEN (*rises*): My dear girl . . .

CLEMENTINE (*embarrassed because she perceives Eva's indifferent attitude*): It's Mr. Merzen, child, you know . . .

MERZEN: . . . The young lady will scarcely remember me anymore. (*Looks at her with unanticipated satisfaction.*)

EVA (*coldly*): Oh, I do. Two years ago you used to come often to see papa.

CLEMENTINE: Imagine, Mr. Merzen is hesitant to stay with us . . .

MERZEN (*politely*): I am afraid that I might be a bother to you, Miss Eva.

EVA (*disdainfully*): To me?—I have nothing to say around here, Mr. Merzen. (*To Clementine*) Did you want something, Mama? . . .

CLEMENTINE (*at a loss*): I just wanted . . . I just wanted to ask you if you would mind looking after dinner, we just can't depend on Anna at all . . .

EVA: I'll get to it right away. (*With a slight nod of her head toward Merzen, exits.*)

MERZEN (*continuing to look at her as she leaves*): Until later, Miss Eva.

*After the door has closed behind Eva, Merzen remains standing with a dazed expression. Mrs. Girding notices it and smiles secretly—then speaks flatteringly.*

CLEMENTINE: Well, Mr. Merzen, may we hope to call you our guest?—Complete with room and board; of course, only if it's not too modest for you—because things are very simple with us, quite ordinary—but we want to offer you everything in our power.—I'm sure Girding has a few good cigars in the house, presents, of course, presents . . .

MERZEN (*his eyes still directed toward the door*): Well, well, well . . . (*Distracted*)

CLEMENTINE: Will you stay then? Will you? . . .

MERZEN (*distractedly*): Listen, she's really gotten beautiful, your daughter (*correcting himself*) Miss Eva . . . (*thoughtfully*) quite enchantingly beautiful! . . .

CLEMENTINE (*acts embarrassed*): Oh, please, please . . .

MERZEN (*looking up*): Really! (*Pulling himself together*) What were you saying earlier, dear Mrs. Girding?

CLEMENTINE: I was asking if you would do us the honor? . . .

MERZEN: Yes, if I wouldn't intrude, I'd like to!

CLEMENTINE: Intrude?

MERZEN: But will Miss Eva . . .

CLEMENTINE: Oh please, she'll be overjoyed when she hears . . . But will you be satisfied with the room?

MERZEN (*without looking around*): Certainly, certainly—absolutely. If I could just ask you for some soap and water. I would like to wash up a bit before dinner. You know how dusty you get from traveling . . .

CLEMENTINE (*busily*): Of course—immediately! (*Wants to leave.*)

MERZEN: Ah—what I wanted to say, Mrs. Girding—I—I congratulate you on having such a daughter. (*Shakes her hand.*)

CLEMENTINE (*with a flattering smile*): You are much too kind, much too kind—we are completely at your service . . . (*bowing, exits.*)

MERZEN *looks after her a moment. Then laughs. Walks forward to the dinner table and sits down in Girding's chair. Makes himself comfortable. Lights a cigarette, leans back, and hums a song.*

*Curtain*

## ACT TWO

*The scene is the same as in the previous act. The family is again at breakfast. This time Hans, who later gets up in order to go to school, is also present. Eva gets up soon after him. Then Merzen,*

*Girding, and Clementine remain together. Instead of the green cloth-covered couch, a badly made bed is in the background.*

*The characters are seated as follows: Girding in his easy chair, Merzen on his right, Clementine to the left, Eva with her back to the audience. Hans walks up and down the room with his hands behind his back.*

CLEMENTINE (*annoyed*): Now sit back down, Hans; this constant getting up while others are eating—it's rude!

HANS: I can't stay hunched up there all the time. I have to repeat one more lesson in my head, and when I'm sitting down, I can't think.

GIRDING: He's right, that boy—was always the same thing with me—never could learn anything by heart unless I was walking back and forth! Don't know why it happens, but that's the way it is.

HANS (*interrupting*): Simple: when you sit still, the mind sits still, too . . . Ha ha ha . . . (*Nobody laughs; Hans keeps on walking.*)

GIRDING: Well, was everything alright for you, my dear Merzen?

CLEMENTINE: You're a little late in asking, Girding. I inquired quite some time ago.

MERZEN (*who reluctantly takes his eyes away from Eva*): Oh excellent, slept very well . . . But you, Miss Eva, you can't boast of the same thing—or can you? You stayed up late; the light in your room—stayed on until midnight. There through the crack in the door—you *are* my neighbor, aren't you?

EVA (*evasively*): That is my room.—I'm not used to going to bed early.

MERZEN (*intimidated*): Oh?—

GIRDING: But you should go to bed earlier, Eva dear. You don't look well at all.—

CLEMENTINE: Oh, come now—it's the light.

HANS (*at the back of the stage, puts on his winter coat now, picks up his books, and near the door, says*): Bye—

CLEMENTINE: Can't you come and say good-bye properly?

GIRDING: Let him be, otherwise he'll be late. Mr. Merzen will excuse him, I'm sure. Good-bye, Hans.

MERZEN (*nonchalantly*): Bye!—

CLEMENTINE: He gets really touchy at times because of all the work, that boy!—It's simply too much.

GIRDING: Nonsense! I'm all for it—my children should learn something!—Don't want to blame my father, God rest his soul, but if he had made me study more, Lord knows things would have turned out differently! Well—that's over and done with. But my children, oh . . . the boy, he'll finish high school, and you, Eva, well, you've certainly learned something, too! She plays the piano, Mr. Merzen!

MERZEN: Hmmm! (*With satisfaction*)

CLEMENTINE: Yes, she can play something for you sometime, too.

EVA: But, Mama, you know how long it's been since I've touched a key.

CLEMENTINE: And we also had her learn French, and she can read English, too . . .

GIRDING: Yes—I've always said—education comes first.—The person who has a general education has the whole world open before him, don't you agree?

MERZEN: Yes, and it's becoming more important every day if you want to accomplish something. It's the trend today. Everybody aspires to so much. Even women are getting their doctorates!—What are we coming to?—Do you think it's right, Miss Eva, that women should emancipate themselves to the point where they usurp occupations fit only for men?—

EVA: I don't know if it's right or not, Mr. Merzen.—I don't like it. A woman belongs at her stove and sewing machine. And when she does something else, she will neglect her duties . . .

MERZEN: You prescribe a very limited circle of activity for women.

EVA: Better to do big things on a small scale than to . . .

CLEMENTINE: My God, who's ever heard you talk so smart?

GIRDING: Always knew she was a clever girl . . .

EVA *gets up.*

CLEMENTINE: Well?

EVA: I have things to do in the kitchen, Mother.

GIRDING: You never give yourself time to rest, Eva, not for a moment!

CLEMENTINE: Don't go putting that stuff in her head, Girding. The way she lazes around the whole day . . .

EVA *exits slowly through the middle door.*

CLEMENTINE (*watches her until she is gone*): You must excuse her for leaving again like that; sometimes she's a bit strange.

MERZEN (*absentmindedly*): Please—please . . . (*To Girding*) Now to get back to our discussion . . . from last night . . .

CLEMENTINE: May I pour you just a little more coffee? Or don't you like our coffee? Mrs. Geschke, the counselor's wife, loves to drink it here.—I measure it out just right, she says—may I, then?

MERZEN: No, thank you. I don't like coffee.

CLEMENTINE: Don't like coffee—well, it's primarily for us women. Gentlemen prefer beer.—How do you like our beer?

MERZEN: It's good.—But I wanted to get around to our important business . . .

CLEMENTINE: Isn't it getting late?—Don't you have to leave now, Girding?

GIRDING (*looking at his watch, uneasy*): Yes, I really do, right away, right away—how time flies!

CLEMENTINE (*continuously winking at Girding*): You'll have to excuse—Girding.—He must be on time.

MERZEN: But your office doesn't open until nine. It's hardly a quarter after eight—therefore.

CLEMENTINE: My, how thoughtless of you, Girding. I ask you— you didn't even offer Mr. Merzen a cigar—and they taste best —after coffee . . . Right?—Yes, that's one thing I know. My father, God bless him, he always insisted on it! Dear God! he always said—I can still hear him—if I couldn't have my stogie . . . if I couldn't have it . . .

MERZEN (*perfunctorily, while Girding holds the cigars out to him; he takes one*): Thank you. (*Lights it calmly, blows two large clouds of smoke out through his pursed lips.*)

*Clementine squirms back and forth uncomfortably in her chair, Girding continues to look at his watch.*

MERZEN: Now, my dear Mrs. Girding, please be so kind as to leave me alone with your husband for a little while; we have important things to discuss.—

CLEMENTINE (*frightened*): Oh, by no means. For heaven's sake. Girding has no secrets from me. Right, Girding—right?

GIRDING *nods, crushed.*

MERZEN: I must insist.—

CLEMENTINE: No, no, not at all, I won't allow you two to tire yourselves out with such things so early in the morning.

MERZEN *motions exasperatedly and stamps his foot nervously.*

CLEMENTINE: Is it perhaps only what you were talking about last night.—Well, there's plenty of time for that . . . surely.

MERZEN (*almost rudely*): No, it's urgent!—It's quite urgent, my dearest Mrs. Girding. (*To Girding*) I must speak to you alone, make that clear to her . . .

GIRDING: Listen (*timidly*) leave us, Clementine . . . leave us—

CLEMENTINE (*offended*): Well, it's fine with me.—

MERZEN: We really must get on with it . . .

CLEMENTINE: Of course! (Scornfully) Enjoy yourselves, gentlemen! (*Exits slowly through the center door, still listening.*)

GIRDING (*keeps looking at his watch*): Now it's really getting late . . .

MERZEN: I won't take much of your time, my dear Mr. Girding. We will have reached an agreement in five minutes. The matter is you see, merely as follows: you must pay me this month what you still own me.—This trifle won't cause you any hardship.— You were able to give your family a summer vacation in the country—or were you perhaps invited? . . .

GIRDING (*confused*): Invited?? Where—I . . .

MERZEN (*satisfied, smiling*): I see.—Well, then, as I said before, you were able to give your family a summer vacation in the country, a sure sign that things aren't going so badly with you anymore.—

GIRDING *more and more crushed, stares stupidly ahead.*

MERZEN: If I were not so certain of all this, my dear Mr. Girding—

GIRDING (*tonelessly*): I don't—have—a penny—

MERZEN: Oh—no, no, don't make this whole affair so difficult for me and for yourself. Pay me today . . .

GIRDING: Sir—I—can't . . .

MERZEN: Alright, the four or five days I'll still be here, I'll give you that much more time . . .

GIRDING (*shouting in a high-pitched voice*): Can't do it, I can't —not today, not tomorrow, not the day after tomorrow . . .

MERZEN (*lightly, holding back his anger*): I know you like to have your little joke, my dear Girding.

GIRDING: May God punish me—if I am not completely serious . . . I . . .

MERZEN (*in a different tone of voice*): Alright, then let's be serious. (*Takes a long puff from the cigar.*) Fine.—You know, as a man of honor, that you must pay your debts when they fall due. Don't you know that? You know that I have overlooked this matter three times in the past, merely because of my personal esteem for you.

GIRDING (*who grasps new hope*): My dear friend . . .

MERZEN: You know all that. Now hear this as well: this time I will not move from here until you have paid me your debt.

GIRDING *winces.*

MERZEN (*with a deadly, icy voice*): I will use any means— understand—any means in order to finally, finally obtain my money and my rights . . .

GIRDING: Any means?—

MERZEN: Exactly.

GIRDING (*agitated*): You mean? . . .

MERZEN (*quietly*): The courts, seizure of your belongings.

GIRDING: Holy Mother of God!—

MERZEN (*smiling*): I know you won't let it get that far . . .

GIRDING: Sir, I *can't.*

MERZEN: Can't, can't . . . this eternal "can't"!

GIRDING: If out of charity you could give me just one more chance! (*Folds his hands and is about to kneel down before him.*)

MERZEN (*still calm*): No play-acting, Girding, this sort of behavior leaves me rather cold.

GIRDING (*still with folded hands*): Have pity on these old grey hairs! . . .

MERZEN *shrugs his shoulders.*

GIRDING: On my children—on Eva!—

MERZEN: On little Miss Stuck-up? Who looks down on me all the time? (*All his wounded passion for Eva breaks through.*) On this girl who acts as though nobody in the world were good enough for her; who thinks that just because she has a pretty face . . . because . . .

GIRDING: God, God! . . .

MERZEN: No, no, my dear fellow—for that girl, for *that* girl I would have done anything . . . but such treatment, never in my life . . .

GIRDING: Dear Merzen!

MERZEN: This little Miss Stuck-up! It's really too laughable. It would even give me pleasure for her to find out . . .

GIRDING: My God!

MERZEN (*growing excited and then continuing icily*): For her to find out that her father . . .

GIRDING (*fearfully*): That . . .

MERZEN (*gets up slowly and speaks the following words very coldly and slowly as he looks sharply at Girding*): That her father, the father of this arrogant girl, is a—thief.

GIRDING (*flaring up, clenches his raised fists in helpless rage*): Sir! (*His voice rasps this out, and then he sinks back in his chair.*)

MERZEN (*his hands behind his back and his head high, he begins to walk up and down arrogantly*): Ha ha ha! Don't be so indignant, my dear friend. You see, we have a good memory. Perhaps a better one than you.—

GIRDING *sits there with his hands clasped in front of his face and groans from time to time.*

MERZEN: And now I hope, Girding, that you will realize I have more than enough ammunition against your silly "can't" and that you will be sensible.—Anyway, I will be lenient. Today is Tuesday. Now listen: (*softly*) Wednesday, Thursday—Friday —(*aloud*)—alright, Friday night the money must be in my hands, otherwise . . .

GIRDING: Otherwise?—

MERZEN (*with venomous humor*): Otherwise your halo will be inexorably lost—you man of honor . . .

GIRDING *gasps for breath.*

MERZEN: Well, that settles that!

GIRDING (*getting up, his hands raised*): Merzen!

MERZEN: Please, my dear Girding, don't trouble yourself . . . I think it's time for you to go to the office—I certainly wouldn't want to detain you.—

GIRDING (*remains standing helplessly a while before him. Then he goes to the coat-rack; groaning, he puts on his coat and wants to leave. At the door he turns around once more):* Merzen!

MERZEN: Hm! Leaving already? Bye, Girding—bye, my dear fellow, enjoy yourself . . .

GIRDING *staggers out.*

MERZEN *his hands in his pockets, he walks up and down in the room, whistling and smoking.*

CLEMENTINE *comes in immediately after Girding leaves the room.*

MERZEN *does not notice her.*

CLEMENTINE (*clearing her throat*): Hm.

MERZEN (*turns around*): Oh—it's you!—

CLEMENTINE: Yes, me, Mr. Merzen—(*jokingly as she bows*)— only me. (*Acts amazed as she looks around.*) What, Girding's gone already?—

MERZEN: Yes, he just left.

CLEMENTINE (*probing and sly*): Well, did the gentlemen come to an agreement?

MERZEN (*casually*): Oh yes.

CLEMENTINE: Wonderful, wonderful! There's nothing like harmony, Mr. Merzen. Right? That's the rule for me. Above all, no arguments. That's what I've always preached to my children.—Listen, I've always said to them. No squabbling! And especially Eva, she's got a quarrelsome streak in her! (*Laughs.*) Oh yes. (*Embarrassed*) Well, Mr. Merzen—how— how do you like our daughter?

MERZEN (*looks up, astonished*): Very much—very much . . .

CLEMENTINE: That's flattering!

MERZEN (*thoughtfully*): She is very pretty.

CLEMENTINE: Yes, that's what everyone always says. Just like her mother, they say, when I was young, of course—I mean, now— now . . .

MERZEN: Hm.—

CLEMENTINE: —Well—what I wanted to say! What I really wanted to say . . . You must excuse me, I wanted to have a word in confidence with you . . .

MERZEN: With *me*?

CLEMENTINE: Of course! So if you'll permit me . . .

MERZEN: I'm anxious to hear what you have to say.

CLEMENTINE: I'll start right off so you won't get "overanxious."
I'll begin right in the middle.—Would you care to sit down a
while?

MERZEN: Thank you.—Been sitting the whole time.

CLEMENTINE: Well then, I'll sit down, there. (*Sits in Girding's
chair.*) Alright: it's about Eva.—I've been complaining right
along about how pale and green the girl is, like an unripe
lemon. Must be she has some kind of secret worry—I've always
said to myself. And I've been watching for a long time. Now
I've figured it out . . .

MERZEN (*stopping in front of her*): Yes, but forgive me, why are
you telling *me* all this . . .

CLEMENTINE (*laughs*): Why you? You need to ask that?
(*Laughs.*) Imagine! (*Laughs.*) That's exactly it, that is exactly
what I've found out.—

MERZEN: What?

CLEMENTINE: All right, one, two, three—out with it: the girl is
in love—with you!—(*Laughs.*)

MERZEN: Whaaat?

CLEMENTINE: It's as I say—just as I say.

MERZEN: Mrs. Girding—no, enough of this joking.

CLEMENTINE: Joking am I—joking, do you think I'm joking? Do
I look like I'm joking? Bless my soul . . . bless my soul! I'm
only laughing because it's so funny, the whole thing! But it's
true!—I tell you—the girl is crazy about you . . .

MERZEN: Oh, Mrs. Girding, I just don't know . . .

CLEMENTINE: Don't know? Well, that's why I'm telling you, so
that you will know!

MERZEN: Miss Eva has not exactly been treating me as if . . .
as . . . if . . . I meant something to her . . .

CLEMENTINE: You think I don't know my own daughter? Please,
I ask you, I ask you now. I know her like the back of my hand.
—(*Laughs.*) Well, you really are something!—You haven't
seen that this is just because she's bashful—it's all because of
that . . .

MERZEN: All . . . because of that . . .

CLEMENTINE: Well, of course. She's crazy about you. From
morning till night . . .

HANS (*comes storming in*): Damned mess . . . (*Throws his book*

*to the left, his coat to the right, and stops in the middle of the room with his hands in his pockets; sullen face.*)

CLEMENTINE (*putting her hands on her hips*): You rotten brat, can't you come into the room properly?

HANS: Ah—leave me alone!—

CLEMENTINE: Now I ask you (*to Merzen*) this is the way his father has brought the rascal up! (*To Hans*) Just wait. What's the matter with you?

HANS (*rudely*): —Damn it all!

CLEMENTINE (*walks toward him with her hand raised*): You stop that right now—shame on you!—Aren't you ashamed to act that way in front of our visitor? He'll have a fine impression of you!—I suppose you got in trouble again?

HANS: How could I know that he would give me a test today, that stupid ass, that . . .

CLEMENTINE: You keep on like this, and you'll end up on the gallows.—You'll see. (*To Merzen*) Please excuse this. (*More softly*) It's impossible to talk with the boy in here. And I want to tell you something else . . . my, oh my—so you didn't know a thing about it—good heavens . . . these men—these men—completely blind—I have to go out anyway. Come along with me for a bit, won't you?—

MERZEN *nods. Takes his hat and coat.*

CLEMENTINE: Well, you're in for a surprise! It's really something, really something!—

MERZEN (*at the door*): Well?—

CLEMENTINE (*still rushing back and forth*): Good Lord, yes, my hat, I left it out in the kitchen—and my jacket too . . . You could lose your head in all this . . . (*She nods to him confidentially.*) Well, well, come with me, dear sir, let's go . . .

MERZEN *goes ahead, she follows—both leave.*

HANS: Well, mama's upset again today. But he certainly is a nice fellow, that Merzen! So well-dressed.—I'd really like to go out with him again—like yesterday! But I've still got this thing on my mind. That stupid test—And that crazy, rotten . . .

EVA *has entered, approaches from the door on the right, slowly and with uncertain steps.*

HANS: Well?! You look great again today. Like someone who just crawled up out of the grave. What's happened to you, Eva?—

EVA *sighs.*

HANS: Oh dear! Oh my!—and always this squawking. You know what you act like all the time? You know? Like some old pump. It goes like this all the time, too (*imitates*) oh—oh—oh!—If I lived the way you do, day in, day out, nothing to do—I certainly wouldn't look like that—

*The doorbell rings. Eva winces visibly.*

HANS: Just look, you jump as if you saw a ghost—that silly little bell goes through you like a knife.

EVA (*shaking*): Is Anna out there?

HANS: Don't know.

EVA: Or mother?

HANS (*just as unconcerned*): Don't know.

*It rings again.*

EVA: Well, go and see.

HANS: Who could it be? Some beggar . . .

*Walks slowly to the back of the stage. As he gets near the door, Eva grabs him and pushes him away.*

EVA: Wait, I'll . . . I'll go myself. (*Exits.*)

HANS: You know what's really wrong with you, sis? . . . It's really too funny! (*Listening*) shh! Who's that talking, it's a man's voice . . . And Eva's talking to him.—He's coming, who can it be? (*Walks quickly to the door on the right, sticks his head out after he has entered the adjoining room.*)

*The center door opens and Dr. Bauer comes in. A youthful, good-looking man with thick, brown hair; he wears his beard short, shaved to a line level with his mouth. Elegantly dressed. He speaks self-consciously and with some embarrassment, but his strong, honest qualities shine through nevertheless. Eva comes in behind him.*

HANS: (*softly, still in the doorway*): Now who in the world is—this?—Aha, Bauer! So this is what the letter meant! (*Slams the door.*)

EVA *looks around nervously.*

BAUER *keeps moving the tip of his umbrella across his shoes.*

EVA (*hesitatingly*): . . . did you . . . get—my letter?

BAUER: I did. (*He tries to sound nonchalant and politely cool.*)

EVA: Why haven't you come for such a long time?

BAUER: Eva . . . Miss Eva . . . Eva . . . you know, my work. So much work. You have to work incessantly, otherwise you can't get ahead. (*Keeps on talking in order to change the subject.*) I am not one of those lucky people who finds all the roads smooth and is welcomed with open arms. I'm a born fighter. I have to work in order to succeed, and when I've succeeded, work to keep it. There is so much envy, so much jealousy, so much arrogance and vanity in our circles. It's so hard to struggle against such enemies!—And there you sit from morning till night over your books, searching, probing, toiling away, toiling away (*breaking off suddenly, curtly*) Ah!—

EVA: . . . and with all this to do, you didn't find time to come and see us even once in two years?

BAUER: Well, it's difficult. I live far away, and the lectures—

EVA: Of course—way over on the other side of town.

BAUER: Yes—well—you see—

EVA (*in sudden passionate intensity*): Fritz!

BAUER *startled.*

EVA (*rushes up to him and throws her arms around his shoulders*): Fritz! Don't look away. Tell me! Don't you feel anything for me anymore?

BAUER (*softly caressing her hair*): Poor Eva!

EVA (*looking up*): Poor?! Then it's true?

BAUER: What?

EVA: That you're getting married!

BAUER: Yes. (*Calmly*)

EVA (*tears herself free—rushes to the corner of the room as if to get as far away as possible from Bauer. She remains standing there, leaning against the cupboard*): Who is she?

BAUER: My God, calm down . . . your health!

EVA: What do you care about my health? Who? . . .

BAUER: Meta von Beiern . . .

EVA: Ha, ha, ha (*shrill laughter*) the banker's daughter?—

BAUER: That's the one.

EVA (*bursts out in shrill laughter*): So this is what you really
are! You who preached to me day after day about the gospel of
self-denial and disregard for money? And now you sell yourself, your ability, your love, your like, for a hefty dowry, a villa,
and a carriage . . . (*Shrill laughter*) You!

BAUER: But I beg your pardon, please, who says . . . that it isn't
love?

EVA: Who says it? I *feel* it!

BAUER: But I assure you . . .

EVA (*firmly*): You're lying!

BAUER: Eva!

EVA: I swear you're lying! Because—because you love me!

BAUER: Hm!

EVA: It's true, isn't it? Yes, yes, yes! You can't deny it, you've
told me so thousands and thousands of times. And you said it
so sweetly, so lovingly! *That* was the truth! And the truth can
never become false—because there is only *one* truth . . . You
—you love me! (*She rushes over to him and embraces him
again.*)

BAUER *tries to answer.*

EVA (*everything in feverish haste*): Don't talk! Not if it's going
to hurt me. Just for now let me think, just for this second, that
you love me. Don't let your cruel words destroy my bright
little dream. Fritz! It's just not possible. See, you were gone.
I didn't call! I trusted you. I said to myself: he'll come. He'll
come when the time is right. Because he's a man.—Always,
always I've thought of the time—when you'd come back and
say: Eva, I've come to take you away—forever! . . . And now
you're here—and, and . . . (*She leans forward and looks up
into his face.*) No, your eyes really have changed, completely,
completely changed—Your whole face—yes—and the way
you're dressed! Go on, Fritz, get rid of all this. You're just
playing a role. You remember, in your loden jacket and your
Rembrandt hat—the way you used to . . . (*becoming childish*)
It's a joke, a cunning joke! Oh, I know my Fritz! Dear old
Fritz. Put all this aside and come (*coaxing*) come on, we'll be
our old selves again . . . (*Sulking*) But you look so serious.
Ohh, so terribly serious! What's the matter, Fritz—what . . .

(*Suddenly, as if waking up, she puts her hands over her face and breaks out in wild sobs.*) But it's really over . . . All over! —(*Cries.*)

BAUER (*embarrassed*): Eva, Eva, my God, I can't stand to see you cry!! Eva (*falls to her knees, still crying, and embraces him violently*): Don't go away from me! Don't go!

BAUER: But . . .

EVA: Don't go! I'll, I'll die—if you leave me! (*She collapses while kneeling and continues sobbing so that her whole body is trembling.*)

BAUER (*stands by helplessly; one can see the deep emotion which he tries to suppress*): But Eva, please—pull yourself together —pull yourself together . . . If I'd known . . .

EVA (slowly *gains control over herself, dries her tears, gets up slowly*): I'm sorry. I guess I got a bit excited.—After all, I don't have the right . . . (*Walking forward with heavy steps, broken but with composure*) Accept my good wishes for . . . (*Her voice falters.*)

BAUER *takes her hands in his and presses them tightly.*

EVA (*smiling amid her tears*): No, my dear friend, I won't let you go yet! Come sit here.—Over here.—(*She indicates a chair to him; she herself sits back in Girding's easy chair.*) Well—and now let's talk about ourselves—as if we were speaking of two strangers . . .

BAUER (*reproachfully*): Eva!

EVA (*smiling*): Don't worry, my friend, all that's over now . . . (*In a light tone*) So you're getting married? Is she young, pretty—charming?

BAUER (*evasively*): Very young.

EVA: Oh?

BAUER: Around seventeen.

EVA: Is that all!—Hm!—Will you be living in town?

BAUER: We haven't actually talked about it yet.

EVA (*suddenly but nonchalantly*): —Tell me—my friend, don't you feel *anything at all for me anymore*?

BAUER *says nothing.*

EVA: Be frank . . .

BAUER *gives a sign of his concern.*

EVA: Don't worry. I'm your friend and I'm very understanding. (*She smiles wearily.*)

BAUER: So be it. Eva! I like you a great deal, a great deal . . . only . . .

EVA (*again in an excited tone of voice, as previously*): Only?

BAUER: —You'll get upset.

EVA: No, no, I'm really very, very calm . . .

BAUER: Only one thing came between us, something that touches me like ice . . .

EVA: And with, with . . . your bride—it's different for you—for you—right? . . .

BAUER: Yes.

EVA: Do you know what it is?—

BAUER: No.

EVA: I do.

BAUER: You?—

EVA: Shall I tell you what it is?

BAUER: Indeed, I'm amazed . . .

EVA: You see, poor uneducated Eva (*she tries to be funny again*) —now all of a sudden she can unravel problems which rack the brain of the learned doctor.—(*Serious, almost visionary*) You know what it is? The early frost!—

BAUER: What?—

EVA: I always knew that one day you'd come and say: there's an icy air about you . . . You see (*rapidly*) you know my youth was hard. I grew up caught between my father's discontent and my mother's rudeness.—I went to school and secretly read all kinds of books which stirred my imagination. My spirit was passive and tended toward the fanciful, you know: that's how it came about that I readily listened to the intoxicating whispers of a boy. It was more to escape my situation and to experience what was in the books, than out of an inclination, that I ran away with him. One hour after the departure, remorse set in! I saw everything in the stark, grey light of day, and found vulgarity instead of romance, baseness and villainy instead of love . . . that was harsh!—The train barely came to halt at the next stop when I jumped out and ran, ran the whole day long through the woods. I had remained pure in body and

soul. I had strayed; but just in time—my eyes had been opened.
I went back home.—Everything will be all right again, I
thought.—But I was bitterly deceived. My father welcomed me
with contempt, my mother with a beating.—And in spite of my
sincere repentance, my begging, my desire for forgiveness, I
did not succeed. Never—not even today.—I was a whore. Even
in my mother's eyes . . .

BAUER (*shocked*): Eva!

EVA: *Yes*, even my *mother* thought badly of me. I had to listen to
terrible things! They suspected that I had penetrated into the
mystery of love, and they repeated thousands of words, which
I was able to listen to because I did not understand them. But
they became clearer. All the sweet secrets which sound so
tender in the language of love were hurled in my face with
barbaric brutality! How I suffered!—And on the street, the
people nudged one another and muttered . . . and I knew what
they were whispering: the whore! And so I lived and suffered,
suffered more than the martyrs whose pictures they adorn with
palms and honor with prayers.—For I knew that I was pure.
And this consolation deep within me washed away all the in-
sults from my soul . . .

BAUER (*admiringly*): You, Eva, you have borne all this!

EVA: Why are you so astonished?—Wasn't I forced to?—But,
you see, now comes the answer to your question.—All the
bitter, harsh words, my false step and the terrible experience
sank into my heart: *"The Early Frost."*—And that's what
makes you feel the cold. That is the curse of my youthful
mistake—the curse which will never be lifted!—You see,
when I got to know you, to love you—I was very miserable.
I had begun to believe the people who scolded, despised, and
slandered me. I thought I really was bad. I had given up on
myself!—Then you came along! How wonderful you were!—
You came to me free of any prejudice.—"I love you," you
said—and then: "Is it true, what the people say?"—And I
explained it all to you.—And you were good. You were a
strong, proud oak on which I could climb up to the light, to the
light!—Oh, I was blissfully happy!—But the early frost remained with me.—You see, and this has been my misfortune.
—You didn't notice it. And then you met her. The one who

radiates the rosy fragrance of sheltered, untarnished youth . . . And then you felt the cold that emanates from me . . .

BAUER (*tries to hold back his emotion*): Poor, poor, dear Eva.

EVA: No, no pity! I am too—too—perhaps too proud for that. And after all—it had to turn out this way . . .

BAUER: You are so good, and I stand here before you like a criminal, Eva!—There's something inside me telling me to go back to you.—

EVA: It's an illusion.—

BAUER: No, no Eva, a voice . . .

EVA: Don't be sentimental, Fritz.—You're happy, aren't you?—

BAUER: Happy?—

EVA (*quickly*): And now, go, go . . .

BAUER: Already?

EVA: Yes, you must, my dear. Your bride will be waiting for you.

BAUER: It's so difficult. May I come back again.

EVA: If you need some friendly advice: yes! or (*fearfully*) better —don't come! Don't come! I want what's best for us—for both of us!—Believe me!—Hm! What am I saying? You won't be thinking of me anyway until . . .

BAUER: I will . . .

EVA: But you shouldn't. Now, go.

BAUER: Good-bye, Eva.—

*They take each other by the hand and remain thus for a while. Then Bauer loses his composure. He embraces her violently. They kiss. Then he tears himself away and goes to the door.*

BAUER: Good-bye!

EVA: Forever!

*Bauer goes to the door; just as he is about to open it, Clementine comes in with Merzen. She stops at the threshold, puzzled.*

CLEMENTINE: Ah.

BAUER *bows.*

CLEMENTINE: What an unusual honor! The doctor! Well, how are you? Thought you were God knows where off at the North Pole—or someplace else.—(*Turning to Merzen*) Ah—the gentlemen don't know each other! Pardon me—pardon me— (*introduces*) Dr. Friedrich Bauer, our dear friend Mr. Merzen. (*Both bow.*) Well, it was nice of you to find your way back to us. May we congratulate you? Congratulations! Congratulations!—You will be introducting us to your bride soon, I hope?—

BAUER: Certainly—certainly. Forgive me, Madam, my time today is somewhat—limited.

CLEMENTINE: I can imagine! There's plenty to do! Right? Shopping and visits!—Well, I don't want to keep you. Come and see us again sometime soon, Doctor.

BAUER *bows to Clementine, then slightly to Merzen.*

CLEMENTINE: Bye, Doctor!

BAUER *bows to Eva.*

EVA *who tries to keep her composure, nods to him.*

BAUER *exits.*

CLEMENTINE (*to Merzen with emphasis*): Don't you have something you want to take care of, my dear Mr. Merzen?

MERZEN: Yes, indeed. I have an important errand. Until later.— (*Merzen leaves.*)

CLEMENTINE: He's become quite a dandy, this darling of yours!—

EVA: Mother!

CLEMENTINE: Well, what do you say now, you goodhearted little ninny? Hm!? Now the gentleman is looking for a nice rich little bride—and you, you're left in the lurch for the second time—so there!—For a little love affair, of course, you were good enough for him—certainly! He has experience in that line, he certainly does! . . . (*Goes over to her and takes her by the hand.*) Now, Eva, listen—I have to have a reasonable talk with you. You're not stupid—no, no, my girl—so look here . . . You know: Merzen—likes you very, very much.

EVA *laughs.*

CLEMENTINE: No, no, by my soul, may God punish me on the spot! . . .

EVA (*harshly*): Stop all this nonsense!

CLEMENTINE: It's not nonsense, Eva. Not at all . . .

EVA: I don't want to hear about it, Mother.

CLEMENTINE: Just take it easy, my darling. All you have to do is listen . . .

EVA (*scornfully*):Have to? (*Laughs.*)

CLEMENTINE (*sits down*): Well . . .

EVA: Oh, leave me alone, Mother . . . (*Wants to leave.*)

CLEMENTINE: Oh no! Stay right there! I have to talk to you. It's urgent. Sit down!

EVA (*yawning, sits down near her mother*): All right—then, go ahead—go ahead, Mother!

CLEMENTINE: Well. First: you mustn't be so rude to Merzen.—

EVA: Merzen again, always Merzen.

CLEMENTINE: Why not, young lady? Everything depends on this man.—Our whole future—your father's, mine, yours—everything . . .

EVA: My God!—

CLEMENTINE: That's why we have to be sensible.—In two days your father will be sitting in the defendant's chair, unless . . .

EVA (*trembling*): Unless? . . .

CLEMENTINE: Well, it depends on you, Eva . . .

EVA: On me?

CLEMENTINE (*coaxing sweetly*): Yes, on you, my darling . . .

EVA: What am I supposed to do? . . .

CLEMENTINE (*in the same tone*): You have to act nice, sweetheart! Very nice.—you must be good to Mr. Merzen and not resist him in anything, anything at all . . .

EVA (*wide-eyed, horrified*): Mother . . .

CLEMENTINE (*angrily*): Well, in short, you'll have to go along with what Merzen wants!

EVA (*rushes with a scream toward her mother, grabs her by the shoulders*): You can't be—serious, you can't be serious—for God's sake . . .

CLEMENTINE (*shakes Eva off*): Don't make such a big fuss over it. Who's hurting you?—Be sensible.

EVA (*with her hands at her temples*): Am I going crazy?—it—it just can't be . . .

CLEMENTINE (*haughtily*): Be quiet!—Such screaming! What's expected of you, anyway?—Just look at how the rich people do it. They get together for the money . . . whether they care for each other or not! Good heavens—things don't always work out so ideally in real life. It's nothing! It'll pass . . .

EVA (*explodes vehemently*): Never—never! Never!—

CLEMENTINE: Alright—then you can lead your father right to court, this minute!—

EVA (*wailing*): My God!

CLEMENTINE: Well now, well now, just be sensible.—

EVA (*hesitatingly*): He wants—wants—to marry me? . . .

CLEMENTINE: Maybe . . .

EVA (*breaking out trembling*): Maybe?! And you, you're supporting him, you . . . (*She throws herself upon her mother with raised, clenched fists.*)

CLEMENTINE (*grabs her by the arm*): What do you expect, you stupid girl!—Tell me.—(*Furiously*) You already ran off with a bum once!—After that you don't have the right to play little Miss Innocence—

EVA (*in helpless rage*): I swear to you, Mother!

CLEMENTINE: Well, poppycock! No matter what you swear to, if a seventeen-year-old girl runs off with a man, my dear, she's got a little experience in that line!—Wouldn't you say!—

EVA *broken, she collapses and sobs.*

CLEMENTINE: It won't do any good! That's the way the world is. —Some people become this, others become that. There have to be whores, too!

EVA (*in a piercing scream*): Mother!

CLEMENTINE: The upper class—the rich, they can preach. They sit at a full table, munching and filling their fat bellies, and use beautiful words to talk about "goodness" and "nobility" and the corrupt masses!—And then they themselves go out in the filthy streets, chasing girls and seducing them and driving them to death and destruction . . . Who do you think makes us bad? —We? Are we the ones? Don't make me laugh! The very ones who always talk about how they improve and educate us! Oh, yes! And if one of the poor people gets hungry or envious and takes a piece of bread from someone who already has too much —then they throw him in jail—because he was hungry—and there he turns bad—bad among the bad—murderers—robbers! And he dies on the gallows! Ha ha ha, on the gallows!—And the ones on top and the wise judges, they think they're cleaning up the evil in the world? The only way they're going to clean it up is by knocking their own skulls together—because that's where it is! Right in there! I don't know anything about politics, and I don't understand the speeches these gentlemen are always giving—but this much I do know, since I have my

wits about me: it's no good this way. And it can't go on!—But
it's still that way now!—That's why you mustn't resist him,
Eva. You were born into this world where corruption is a part of
life. And our dear Lord in his infinite wisdom has everything
all beautifully preordained. This one will be a carpenter, that
one a count, and that one a king—the other one a scoundrel—
well, and you, you he made a whore! Our dear Lord—Stand
up!—

EVA *her spirit broken, obeys hesitatingly.*

CLEMENTINE (*continues in great excitement*): You don't have
to be ashamed in front of people—for a long time now they've
been thinking that you're a loose girl!—Well, God forgive
them. And after all, my oh my! . . . the one above, the Heavenly
Father has really been especially good to you. He could have
made something a lot worse out of you.—What can a daughter
be, when her father is a—

EVA *listens breathlessly.*

CLEMENTINE: When her father is a—thief!

EVA *stares at her mother with dull, umcomprehending eyes.*

CLEMENTINE (*walking over to her*): Well, now it's all out in the
open. Now you can do as you wish. But I think you can see
how far you'll get with honesty! We can't afford to be honest—
if we want to live! I'm not forcing you—I could order you—I
am your mother! But I won't force you. I say to you: do as
you wish. But remember—if you don't do as I told you, your
father will be sitting in jail the day after tomorrow.—Think it
over.—(*About to leave*)

EVA (*embraces her*): Mother!

CLEMENTINE: There, there, my child, don't cry . . .

EVA: It's so horrible!

CLEMENTINE: Well, pull yourself together . . .

EVA: I love father so much . . .

CLEMENTINE: Think it over.

EVA (*looks at her mother for a while in silence, then slowly and
with determination*): I'll—do it!—

CLEMENTINE: You will? Good girl.—(*Again in a harsh voice*)
And the door which leads to your room stays open tonight!—

EVA *trembles.*

CLEMENTINE: Understood?!

EVA (*in a monotone, sobbing*): Yes.—

*She sinks into her mother's arms and sobs so that her whole body trembles.*

*Curtain*

## ACT THREE

*The setting is the same as in the two previous acts. The following morning. The room has been straightened up rather carelessly. The chairs stand in no particular arrangement. On the cupboard and desk everything is messy. Eva is sitting on the unmade bed in a dirty, loose robe, her hair unkempt and her face very pale. She is leaning her head on her hands. After a while, Girding comes through the center door. He looks smaller, more sunken together, more miserable than ever. He walks timidly and does not even notice Eva at first.*

EVA (*raises her head, drops her hands in helpless exhaustion without getting up from the bed*): Good morning, Father.

GIRDING (*looking around*): Eva, dear.—(*Walks toward her, kisses her forehead.*) So pale—so pale! Is something wrong, child?—

EVA (*without looking at him*): Oh no . . .

GIRDING: Did you sleep well last night?

EVA (*nods, then as if recollecting*): No—not really—not well at all.

GIRDING: That's easy to see! Poor child!

EVA *looks at him questioningly.*

GIRDING (*worried*): Won't you go rest a little?

EVA (*sighs*): Yes, I should.

GIRDING (*tenderly*): Go ahead. ·

EVA (*gets up, takes a few steps, stops, turn as if she wants to say something else—father and daughter face each other thus for a while, then Eva puts her arms around him and kisses him vehemently and affectionately*): Father!—(*Tears away and leaves through the door on the right.*)

GIRDING *stares after her for a moment. Then he walks up and down the room, his steps dragging. Finally, still dressed in his overcoat, he drops into his easy chair.*

HANS *comes through the door on the right, whistling, ready to go out.*

GIRDING (*looking up*): Leaving?
HANS: Oh, Father; yes!—
GIRDING: Where to?
HANS: Oh—for a walk. Bye.
GIRDING *nods.*
HANS (*turning back at the door*): You know, Papa, actually this is funny . . .
GIRDING: Hm?
HANS: Really funny.
GIRDING: What's that?
HANS: The way Mr. Merzen sneaked out this morning!
GIRDING (*with unconcealed astonishment*): Out?!
HANS: Yes.—When I woke up, I heard a racket in here. I went through Eva's room. It was empty.—And then I looked through the keyhole . . . And here was Eva sitting on the edge of the bed asleep . . .
GIRDING: Who?
HANS (*blinking his eyes*): Well, Eva.
GIRDING: In here?—That's not true! (*Vehemently*)
HANS: I have good eyes, Father. You know, when I see something . . .
GIRDING: That just can't be . . . (*Trying to control himself*)
HANS: Heavens, she probably helped Mr. Merzen with his packing . . . because he sneaked through the room, his suitcase in his hand . . . Up and gone . . . thought nobody saw him . . . hee hee hee . . . Isn't that funny?
GIRDING *stares ahead apathetically.*
HANS: Really funny—hm, Papa?
CLEMENTINE (*enters from the left*): What's funny?
HANS: He's gone.
CLEMENTINE: Who?
HANS (*draws it out*): Mr. Merzen.

CLEMENTINE (*calmly*): Oh.—Probably had some important business.

GIRDING (*fixes his eye on Clementine. To Hans*): You go on now—we have something to talk about . . .

HANS: On my way! (*Exits whistling.*)

GIRDING (*sternly*): What's wrong with Eva?

CLEMENTINE (*sitting down without looking at him*): What should there be? Nothing.

GIRDING: Clementine, Hans told me that Eva was here on this bed early this morning . . .

CLEMENTINE (*startled*): Nonsense. Whenever that brat comes up with a ridiculous story—you believe every word he says . . .

GIRDING: Ridiculous?

CLEMENTINE: Well, what else? (*Changing the subject*) Why are you already back from the office today, Girding?—

GIRDING: I didn't go to the office.

CLEMENTINE: Not to the office? That's the end of the world. You didn't go to the office. Maybe because you're so glad that Merzen's left? See, you were all ready to give up! And now he's gone, the bum, that bloodsucker Merzen, and you've got your peace and quiet again.

GIRDING: It's all the same to me whether he's here or not.

CLEMENTINE: Don't be stupid! What do you mean?

GIRDING: It's all the same!

CLEMENTINE: Now listen.

GIRDING: I went to the police.

CLEMENTINE: Come now, why would you go there?

GIRDING (*hoarsely*): I turned myself in.

CLEMENTINE *stares at him silently, unable to utter a word.*

GIRDING: Yes, I didn't have the courage to say it out loud, and so I wrote it all down exactly as it happened and told them to take the letter over to the police commissioner, and now I'm waiting until they . . .

CLEMENTINE (*regains her voice*): You stupid ass, you spineless idiot! You coward, you!—That's what you did!—Damn you, I could wring your—(*Wringing her hands uncontrollably*) That's what you did!—You miserable . . . you . . . (*She gasps for breath.*) But I knew all along that you'd throw a monkey-wrench in the works—you . . .

GIRDING (*not intimidated this time*): I did the right thing, Clementine.

CLEMENTINE (*beside herself*): Oh—of course—you're such a great, noble character.

GIRDING: I have rid myself of my guilt—my conscience is clear— I will take the punishment I deserve!—

CLEMENTINE: Ha ha ha! What a man of honor! Take the punishment. And what about me—and what about the children? The children of a thief!

GIRDING: This only has to do with me.

CLEMENTINE: With you? Your grandchildren will still know that their grandfather was a thief, and they'll spit on your grave!— That's the kind of man I married.—That's the kind! Back when my father died and I was left without a penny, if I'd only gone and gotten a police permit and walked the streets at night—it would have been—better—better, I tell you.—And for you—I do everything to get you out of this mess—and you, you throw yourself in jail, you give yourself up!—(*Piercing laughter*)

GIRDING: My conscience demanded it of me. I lay there all night without sleeping and thought about it . . . all night . . .

CLEMENTINE: All night!—

GIRDING: All night!—

CLEMENTINE (*with terrible scorn*): I can tell you a few things about that night, too. Come here.

GIRDING *moves the chair closer.*

CLEMENTINE (*looks around carefully, then with emphasis*): Last night, for you—for *you* . . . your child became a whore.

GIRDING: Clementine!

CLEMENTINE: (*icily*): Ask her yourself!—

GIRDING: Holy Mother of God!—

CLEMENTINE: And he goes and gives himself up!—

GIRDING (*crying*): My little Eva, my little Eva.

CLEMENTINE: Go on and cry! It's too late now.

GIRDING: You did this, woman! (*He jumps up, trembling all over.*)

CLEMENTINE (*grabs him by the arm and hurls him back into his chair*): Coward! Maybe now you'll blame me—because I wanted to save you—and drag you out of the mess—you crawled into. Well, now you're really stuck in it.—(*Makes a sudden decision.*) But I'm going to let you sit in it by yourself. I am the child of decent parents, you know! I won't have anything more to do with a thief! Understand? You'll never see me again!

GIRDING (*moaning*): The children—the children!

CLEMENTINE: You didn't think of them when you stood in the police station—right? They didn't mean a thing to you, your children. Now all of a sudden! Of course! Well, you've already turned your daughter into a whore anyway . . .

GIRDING: This is—too much . . .

CLEMENTINE: You whimpering old woman! . . . It serves you right!—Well, and Hans won't turn out much better. He's already insolent enough. I'm telling you—like father, like son. Remember that. And now good-bye. Have a good time in jail— you'll never see me again as long as you live—not me . . . (*Slams the door. Leaves.*)

GIRDING (*stretches out his hands helplessly*): Clementine! (*Then he collapses and sobs, his hands pressed against his face. In a little while, the doorbell rings. He jumps, murmurs to himself*) The police!—

*Silence. Girding sits in his chair staring vacantly into space. Then: a man's voice outside. Girding gets up, using all his strength to support himself on the arm of the chair.*

ANNA (*sticks her head in*): A gentleman . . . the gentleman who . . .

GIRDING *gestures that he be let in. Looks toward the door with his head bowed and the expression of a cornered deer.*

BAUER (*enters*): My dear Mr. Girding.

GIRDING *still staring vacantly into space.*

BAUER (*closer*): I took the liberty of stopping by—

GIRDING (*in sudden, happy, surprised relief*): Oh, my dear Mr. Bauer.—(*Shakes his hand with both hands.*) Almost didn't recognize you! It's been so long since I've seen you . . .

BAUER: How are you?

GIRDING: I—oh thanks . . . Excuse me, I have to sit down—a little faintness—age affects us all, my friend.

BAUER: Oh, perhaps—but quite gradually, it seems to me.

GIRDING: Please sit down.—To what do we owe the pleasure?—

BAUER: A rather delicate matter.—You know—how highly I always have thought of your daughter, and I have often expressed the serious nature of my affection quite clearly to you. —(*Girding's face clears up more and more.*) You see, Mr. Girding—there came a time when I kept myself away from Eva. I don't know why.—I had met a young girl, found her parents most cordially inclined toward me, and because of the charming and coquettish naiveté of the daughter I became— how shall I say—ensnared and deceived!—And one evening we became engaged.—There was a voice inside me which reproached me . . .

GIRDING (*startled*): Yes, there are voices like that—aren't there?—(*More relaxed*) Excuse me for saying so—but I have felt the same thing.

BAUER (*squeezes his hand*): But the constant parties, the theater, the dinners, the many friends who kept telling me how lucky I was—half out of jealously, half out of admiration—all these things left me no time to really think it over.—The wedding was to take place soon.—Then—yesterday I stood before your daughter. Stood there before her like a scoundrel—like a criminal . . .

GIRDING *starts violently*.

BAUER: And her gentle, sincere words flowed through my soul, and the false, vain feeling within me disappeared—because my love for Miss von Beiern was an illusion.—As soon as I left here, I began to waver. And when I walked into the fashionable salons, and found my fiancée surrounded by all those boring dandies—and saw how she enjoyed the empty jokes—such a feeling of disgust came over me that I couldn't understand how I had been able to tolerate it for so long— how I was so willing to—tie myself to this vain girl for the rest of my life.—I'll be frank: in addition to all this, Meta's father made a remark about the money that I, a less well-off person, would receive—through this marriage.—Well, in short —I asked to be freed from my promise. Meta agreed with a smile . . . and I . . . I . . . Mr. Girding. I have told you all this, told you in every detail, because you are the father of the girl to whom I owe an apology—and whom I wish with all my power to repay for her kindness and constant love . . . Tell me frankly, Mr. Girding, will you give me your daughter's hand in marriage?

*Girding says nothing for a while.*

GIRDING: My God . . .

BAUER: I don't mean to rush you. One thing more:—Don't think that it was irresponsibility that caused me to propose to Meta von Beiern. It was an error of the heart.—An illness. Now I'm cured! I want to do everything for Eva, everything . . .

GIRDING *shakes Bauer's hand, but is unable to utter a word.*

BAUER: Dear Mr. Girding!

GIRDING (*in a soft voice, much moved*): Speak to her yourself— I'll call her.—

*He gets up with great difficulty, and goes to the door on the right, all bent over, his steps dragging. His face darkens. Then he turns around.*

GIRDING (dully): I just want to let you know, Doctor, that every-thing—everything . . . is not as it should be in my house . . .

BAUER *makes a motion with his hand in protest.*

GIRDING: No, no my friend, it's true. So many things happen . . . (*Hesitates.*) Maybe I am not the . . . the man you take me for . . .

BAUER (*stepping closer*): My dear Mr. Girding, I *love* your daughter!

GIRDING (*moved*): God bless you! Well then, I'll send her to you! I'll send her . . . (*He turns around right at the door.*) And— and my blessing as well!—(*With ill-concealed emotion, exits.*)

BAUER *walks up and down nervously, but with a smile of anticipa-tion on his face.*

EVA *comes in, she is startled when she sees Bauer, walks forward with slow steps and downcast eyes.*

BAUER (*warmly stretching out his hands to her*): Eva!—

EVA *stares fixedly at the floor. She does not notice the outstretched hands.*

BAUER: Are you angry with me? Well, you have a right to be! You're probably thinking to yourself: yesterday that—today this.—But many things have happened between yesterday and today!—

EVA (*startled, and then trembling, whispers*): Many, many things!

BAUER: Look at me.

EVA *continues to stare fixedly at the floor.*

BAUER: You see—I was blind! Now I've learned to see. Can you forgive me? I've come to realize—how—how boundlessly I love you! How all the threads of my life are woven into yours! —Yes, yes, I feel it.—It's ecstasy just to be near you . . .

EVA *slowly looks up, but immediately casts her eyes back down again.*

BAUER: You look at me questioningly, searchingly.—Yes, I feel happy near you! No cold at all!—That was an illusion, an awful illusion, a ghost!—

EVA *shakes her head gravely.*

BAUER (*tenderly*): Don't shake your head, Eva—darling Eva! —It's true. My love, the early frost doesn't touch me anymore. The early frost can be melted by the hot, burning fire of overpowering love! . . .

EVA (*hesitatingly, in a different tone from before*): Do you think so?

BAUER: I know it, Eva—the early frost is melting away;—it has already . . . (*Stretches out his arms.*)

EVA: Has already . . . (*Hurries a few steps toward him, with burning eyes—in indescribable, joyful excitement. Two steps before him she stops. Her looks turn gray, her whole body shrinks.*)

BAUER (*shocked*): What's the matter with you?—

EVA: Go, go away!—

BAUER: But tell me!—What is it? Come here. (*Stretches out his arms.*)

EVA (*shaking*): I mustn't!

BAUER: Eva!

EVA: I mustn't—I can't . . .

BAUER: Why? Tell me!

EVA: Because . . . because I'm unworthy—of you . . .

BAUER: You must have a fever, why are you saying these foolish things?—Stop it—(*Wants to draw her to him.*)

EVA: No, no, no!—

BAUER: You want to punish me!

EVA: Fritz!

BAUER: Now be sensible! Don't you love me at all anymore?

EVA: This torment! (*In tears*)

BAUER: All right, what is tormenting you?

EVA (*with superhuman strength, as if in a trance*): Look over there!

BAUER (jokingly): At what?

EVA: Right there! That bed!

BAUER (*also becoming serious because of the tone of her voice*): The bed? So? . . .

EVA (*walks slowly and with tired steps to the corner where the bed is, there she draws herself up. With icy sternness*): Last night in this bed I was a whore.—(*She remains there, pale as a statue.*)

BAUER (*rushes toward her*): Eva!

EVA *stands there motionless with a numb look on her face.*

BAUER (*lets his hands fall*): You're dreaming, child, you're lying! Ha ha ha—That was a good joke.

EVA: Do you want me to swear to it? (*As before*)

BAUER: Don't overdo it, Eva. This can't be! But I have a hot temper—and . . .

EVA (*in a high, strong voice*): I swear it!—

BAUER *as if insane, stares at the girl, then a shock runs through his body, his fists clench, he leaps forward, grabs Eva by the throat and strangles her. Only a slight rattle. Then she sinks down, lifeless. She is lying on the floor beside the bed, her head leaning against the edge of the bedstead. Bauer stares at her and sinks limply onto the bed. He sits there, mumbling softly and softly caressing her blond hair. At the moment of Eva's death, a shot is heard inside to the right. Now Anna storms in from the right and screams.*

ANNA (*from the right side*): Lord have mercy, it's Mr. Girding!—

HANS (*through the center door, breathless*): Police!—

*Curtain*

# Air at High Altitude

*A Play in One Act*

### Characters:

ANNA, *seamstress, twenty-nine years old*
TONI, *her son, six years old*
THE HOUSEKEEPER, *fifty years old*
MAX STARK, *ex-officer, twenty-six years old*

*The individual characters are clearly delineated. Anna, plain in dress and bearing. Everything gives evidence of her transcendence: the calm, clear look; the white, wishless hands. Max Stark, not exactly dandyish, but fashionably modern. Blond with a twirled mustache, possibly a pince-nez. The "Mna" he pronounces very curtly. Toni can be between six and eight years old. Not a "professional" actor, but rather sincere and ardent: a blond little rascal. Everything else is left to the judicious director.*

*Place of the action: Small German town. Plain attic apartment. Time: The present. Shortly before Christmas. Noon. The plain attic room is neat and clean; the small panes in the low window hung with white curtains. The floors scrubbed clean. In the deep alcove of the attic stands the sewing machine. The bed is covered with a flowered cotton blanket, next to it the child's bed, especially pretty with a green, netted-yarn cover pulled back. On the table, the remains of a meal which the old housekeeper is about to remove. Around the table, an armchair covered with black shiny*

71

*leather, and two ordinary wooden chairs. Housekeeper is cleaning off the table. Anna is sitting in the alcove and sewing at the machine.*

HOUSEKEEPER: You really don't eat much, Miss Anna. Just like a bird.

ANNA: But you serve such large portions, Mrs. Baumer.

HOUSEKEEPER (*good-naturedly*): Well, I just tell myself: the boy. Since he's growing . . .

ANNA: He does like to eat. Mornings—well, you know yourself— the giant sandwich he takes with him. And when he comes back from school, he can hardly wait, he's so hungry.

HOUSEKEEPER: And well he should be! My Pepi, when he was little, you should have seen him! With what eyes he used to gobble down the whole bowl . . . Lord, now he's already gotten a position in the world, too. That is, he's with the bank. You know, the big bank in the capital. Yes, and doing very well. And a position of—trust it is, too. Just think of the money that goes through his hands: the *thousands* and the *millions.*—Just think of all that work. Everyday till late in the evening. And sometimes he even stays after closing time. Yes.—But now he'll come home for once and be with us on Christmas. Well, it's only right that he should belong a little bit to his old mother again, too—and . . .

ANNA (*stops sewing*): Yes—then you'll have a nice Christmas. You won't forget the little tree, will you Mrs. Baumer?

HOUSEKEEPER: For our Toni! Forget! Come, come, Miss Anna, you should know me better. I tell you: that Toni, we all love him so much. It's really too . . . ! Yes—on the twenty-third I'll bring you a little tree. Yes. And a few paper chains, too.

ANNA: That's very nice of you.

HOUSEKEEPER: It's nothing. That's left over from our children. We don't need it anymore now. Yes. Well, you don't need anything else, Miss Anna, do you?—Well. (*Gathers up the dishes. While leaving*) Now don't you worry about that tree, leave everything to me. A fine one—I tell you. Bye.

ANNA: Thank you so much, Mrs. Baumer.

HOUSEKEEPER (*in the doorway*): It's nothing, nothing. I keep telling you: for our Toni . . . (*Leaves*)

ANNA *sewing industriously; the machine is audible. Pause. Then voices outside. Pause.*

HOUSEKEEPER (*comes in with a look of surprise and carefully shuts the door behind her*): Miss Anna!

ANNA *doesn't hear, keeps on sewing.*

HOUSEKEEPER: Miss Anna!

ANNA (*without stopping*): Yes?!

HOUSEKEEPER (closer): Someone's here.

ANNA (*looks up*): Work for me?

HOUSEKEEPER: Doesn't look like it, a fancy gentleman.—Yes.—

ANNA: It can't be for here.

HOUSEKEEPER: Yes, yes; (hastily) he said the name exactly. Miss Anna Stark, he said. And he's wearing a fur coat. I think he's a count or something.

ANNA (*getting up, annoyed*): Well, then, Mrs. Baumer, go and say that I receive no one. If possibly work were to be left . . . But no. I receive no one. Say that—please!

HOUSEKEEPER: All right, all right. (*She goes to the door*) I'll say it, yes. (*Opens.*)

MAX STARK *comes in quickly at that same moment.*

ANNA (*startled at first, then rushes toward him with visible joy*): Max! (*She embraces him*)

MAX (*kisses her*): Well . . .

ANNA (*scarcely believing*): You?!

MAX: That's right, little sister. It's me. Mna and—you?

HOUSEKEEPER *who had been standing at the door, exits.*

ANNA (*still holding him*): Is it really possible?

MAX: It required enough effort. Like looking for a needle in a haystack. You've set yourself up rather high.—Haven't you? Rather high; mna.—Let's have a look. (*Looking around*) You're not exactly in splendid circumstances here. But as long as . . .

ANNA *breaks into tears.*

MAX (*impatient*): Mna—Now you're even crying! Mna, little sister, little sister. (*Comforting*)

ANNA (*drying her tears*): How's mother?

MAX: Mother? Fine, thank you. That is to say. So-so . . . yes.

ANNA *listens anxiously.*

MAX: Getting old, too, you know. Nothing of significance. A little pain here and there. We'll all be that way someday. Mna, but until then . . .

ANNA *looks at him with big eyes, questioning.*

MAX: Hm?

ANNA *persists.*

MAX (*guessing it*): Oh yes—father.—Mna yes, quite grouchy at times, too. But so far . . . Well—(*Pause*) Mna, but first of all: What have you been doing? How long has it been since we last saw each other?

ANNA: Over six years.

MAX: Over six . . . ? Really. Yes, yes: two, four, five . . . You may be right. Of course, I was still a lieutenant back then. Wet behind the ears.—(*Pause*) Really bothered me frightfully then, the whole affair. Mna . . . (*In a different tone*) You're somewhat pale, somewhat pale . . .

ANNA: I think it's the light.

MAX: Oh? Perhaps. Now, what I wanted to say. You're getting along—well? Hm?

ANNA: Oh yes. (*Calm*) I am quite content.

MAX: Mna, that's nice. (*Pause.*)

ANNA (*hesitating*): Why don't you sit down, Max.

MAX: Yes. (*Sits down in the armchair.*) Ah! I assume one may smoke in your house? Hm?

ANNA: Of course.

MAX (*takes a cigar from his case*): You know, it's really something. Yes. At our house it's still the same old story: Lord have mercy—the walls! and Lord have mercy—the curtains! It's disgusting.—Mna—old people. (*Lights the cigar.*) Henry Clay—notice the aroma! It'll do you good. You know, the air here isn't much. You actually eat in the same room, don't you?

ANNA (*sits down, smiling*): This is my dining room, where you're sitting, there (*points at the bed*) my bedroom, and there (*points toward the corner*) is my little workroom.

MAX (*puffing*): Well divided. Quite extraordinary. Shows taste. —Well, what do you think of this brand? (*Blows a ring toward her.*) Aroma, hm?

ANNA: Dear Max, I don't under– . . .

MAX: Mna—yes (*puffs*) actually we have something more important to discuss. Hmm.—(*Pause*) First of all, forgive me for
having intruded upon you so quickly without any further respect
toward your hired hand; but ante-chambering out there was of
a somewhat cold nature. Mna and—you know, in certain exceptional cases it is permissible to disregard regulations which
are valid under ordinary circumstances. Mna—well and . . .
(*Twirls his mustache nervously. Suddenly*) Reconquering one's
sister is that kind of exceptional case. Correct?

ANNA *looks at him without understanding.*

MAX (*embarrassed*): Mna . . .

ANNA *still looks at him.*

MAX: Well—That is, you see, the reason for my coming. Besides
my own personal, brotherly affection—of course.—In short, I
was sent by mama . . .

ANNA (*in joyful surprise*): Mother!!

MAX (*dryly*): Yes.

ANNA (*trembling with joy*): Tell me, Max. Mother sent you . . .
and . . .

MAX: Yes, she would have come herself; but—the weather . . .
after all, she has gotten a little sensitive.

ANNA (listening expectantly): Mother? . . .

MAX (takes a long drag on his cigar): Mna: she expects you
to come home for Christmas.

ANNA (*jumps up and embraces him*): Really, Max?

MAX (*dryly*): Yes. Mna. Do you want to?

ANNA (*listening attentively*): Back home, Lord!

MAX: Hm.

ANNA (*standing with folded hands*): How can you even ask? I
do—I do! (*Jubilant*) Mother! How did she say it to you? Tell
me.

MAX (*bored*): Oh God, they've been talking about it at the table
for ages. Back and forth, on and on . . .

ANNA (*timidly*): And father?

MAX: Father? (*Puffs.*) Mna, he'll say: Yes and amen once he
gets to see you.

ANNA: Is he still angry?

MAX: As I told you. He is very grouchy. Being around these old people is truly a cross to bear. Never a moment of peace and quiet.

ANNA *listens, startled and surprised.*

MAX: It keeps starting all over again.

ANNA: Yes—but?

MAX: Does that surprise you? That's the way it's always been. The squabbling.—

ANNA *with a questioning look.*

MAX: About what? God, about this and that and nothing. Every little thing. Irritable they are, these people; you have no idea. And then it always comes back to who has *you* on his conscience.

ANNA (*terrified*): Me?

MAX: Yes, it's ridiculous. Hm? He says she was too good and gave you too much freedom, and she says he spanked you too much. Ridiculous. Ah, I could just . . . You still have it best, you know. So completely on your own. If I could do that!— Mna but after all it's different in your case. Women always understand each other better, and when there are two in the house—then papa is bound to be the loser.

ANNA *silent, staring down into nothingness.*

*Pause*

MAX (*breaking off*):Mna, I'm glad, I'm glad you're going. What I was going to say is that I've pushed the decision rather a lot with mama. After all—hm!—between us: It is absolutely necessary that someone come and mix in for a while. There's such a fatalistic atmosphere. A little fresh air . . . (*Considers.*) Mna, I can tell *you*, you're not a prude. Had another little affair. You know: a girl. God, so in passing . . . A really pretty little thing, quite young.—Mna, just a bit of amusement—and finished. And the little thing takes it wrong and jumps in the water.

ANNA (*wide-eyed*): And . . .

MAX: And what? (*Impudently*) Finished.—Stupidity—Wasn't it?

ANNA (*shocked*): Max?!

MAX (*tugging at his mustache*): Anyway—rather awkward.

ANNA: And you simply . . . ?

MAX: Let's have no sermons, Anna dear. What does it have to do with me, after all? *I didn't tell her to do it.*

ANNA (*marvels at him, then slowly, with emphasis*): You have her on your conscience.

MAX: Yes, yes, I know. Mna, maybe they'll fry me a little longer for it below. Hm? Sunny side up? It doesn't matter . . . Still.

ANNA: Max, I just can't conceive—how you . . .

MAX (*annoyed*): Alright! That's just about enough. It's really boring. To think that such Philistine thoughts are kept here, four flights up.—Matter of taste—By the way, the fact that, in a similar situation, one can do something other than jump in the water—is . . . (*Looks at her meaningfully.*)

ANNA *jumps up.*

MAX: Let's pass over that!

ANNA *goes to the chest-of-drawers and mechanically, absentmindedly, picks up one thing after another.*

MAX (*lightly*): I only told you the whole silly story so that you'd understand why papa and mama . . .

ANNA (*turns*): They know about it?

MAX (*with a certain arrogance*): God yes. Public secret.—That sort of thing gets around. In intimate circles people are beginning to whisper. A kind of—fame. Mna. (*conceited*) It feels pretty good to be in the news a bit from time to time. Hm?

ANNA (*icily*): I don't understand you.

MAX: No?—You know, you'll simply have to talk the old people out of it. Actually, I depend upon them completely. There are a lot of obligations now . . . and papa—between us—is a big Philistine, he would be capable of . . .

ANNA (*aloof*): I should beg for you?

MAX (*gets up*): But my dear sister, you don't understand me, you mistake the situation. I only mean . . .

ANNA (*abrupt*): *I don't think I will understand the parents any-more either—*

MAX: That'll pass.

ANNA (*very seriously*): I don't understand any of you . . .

*Pause.*

MAX (*tosses the cigar butt toward the stove and walks back and forth with his hands behind his back*): Yes—it's the years. (*Yawns.*)

ANNA: Max, I think that something else lies between us besides the years.

MAX *looks at her questioningly.*

ANNA (*grandly*): I have found peace.

MAX: Mhm!

ANNA: Isn't that all we can have on earth?

MAX: Peace?—Yes.—Mna but (*impertinent*) can you heat your stove with it?—Then I find it—as a source of heat, at least—rather inadequate, that peace of yours.

ANNA (*as if she hadn't heard*): There must be an entirely different air down in your houses. An oppressive heaviness. I don't know, I'm not used to it anymore. I can only remember as in a dream that I once breathed it. A long time ago.—And then: in your world you look into walls and—into your neighbors' windows. But *here*—look—far, far across all rooftops. And the sky is much closer here. I often think at night that I could catch the stars with my hand.—Everything is different here. People only come up here through great suffering. Then they either die up here, or—overcome it. And if they overcome it, then they are tired and gentle and peaceful, as after a long illness. And then they are full of forgiveness and charity—and they don't understand what's below anymore—they are so . . . *beyond all suffering.*

*Pause.*

MAX (*listens as if captivated. Then, almost unwillingly, he tears himself away, in the old tone*): Finished?! Mna, that was quite a remarkable performance. You should write novels. That isn't supposed to be the worst thing in the world . . . And, to make a long story short: in response to my generous invitation to rejoin the family circle, the gracious lady condescends, freely and cheerfully—to whistle in my face. Correct?

ANNA (*intimidated*): You shouldn't scoff.

MAX: And you shouldn't play the gracious lady. Graciousness is not quite in your line. (*Looks at his pocket watch*) By the way, it's also getting late. (*Curtly*) Alright, here I stand, sent by your mother to invite you to return to the arms of your parents, et cetera, et cetera . . . Do you want to? Yes or no?—

ANNA (*decidedly*): Yes.

MAX (*somewhat taken aback*): I see-e. Mna, all right. Very nice. That sense of duty of yours has won you to your parents' side after all.

ANNA (*softly*): Don't delude yourself. That isn't it.

MAX: Well then?

ANNA: I have a higher duty.

MAX: Hm?

ANNA: My child.

MAX (*in terror and astonishment*): What?—

ANNA: I think the prospects for little Toni's future will be improved if I . . .

MAX: Then he's alive . . . ? (*More composed*) Mna, that's very nice. You're right. Well, where is the . . .

ANNA: Toni's at school.—Wait till you see him, Max! (*Enthusiastically*) Wait till you see him! (*Fervently*) He's everything I've got.

MAX (*thoughtfully*): I see.

ANNA (*as fervently as before*): He is a good boy and hardworking, too.

MAX: And he's already going to school? Mna, well, that's quite nice. Then little . . . What's his name?

ANNA: Toni.

MAX: Toni? Hm.—Then little Toni will be coming with you?— Mna, yes. Mama will be happy, I'm certain.—Actually, we'd never though of that. Six years . . . That's fabulous, by the way: old Mrs. Fellner (remember?), my landlady when I was a lieutenant— she has always wanted to take care of something like that. We'll give the little scamp to *her*. She has a firm hand, old Mrs. Fellner.—Ha! He'll sprout up with *that old hag*. Perfect. And you're rid of it—

ANNA (*who listens in astonishment; tense, holding herself back*): You think so?

MAX: Of course, little sister. I'm a decent fellow after all, aren't I? Advice right on the tip of my tongue. Old Fellner! I deserve a big hand for that. (*Looks out the window.*) You know, quite aside from the trouble and bother—you couldn't bring something like that home. You know that yourself. Papa is a retired government official, I was an officer—and then we do have certain obligations and cannot offend people.

ANNA (*scarcely able to control herself*): Is that so!?

MAX (*still looking out the window*): Lord, why waste any more words over it; this is strictly a matter of common social grace— consideration, awareness, mna, in a word—honor.

ANNA (*bursting out, so that Max looks around in surprise*): All that is to be found down there? My, what beautiful things you have! You have social consideration and good breeding and culture and honor—and—no heart. (*Laughs scornfully.*)

MAX (*in great astonishment*): Now just one . . .

ANNA (*more quiet and serious*): Don't ever take the trouble to come up here again, Max. It's normally very quiet here. You carry with you discord and hatred and—contempt.

MAX (*hoarsely*): Anna! (*He laughs contemptuously*)

ANNA: Did you want something else?

MAX (*at first speechless*): You're showing me the door? That's the thanks I get. That's just what I've always said. That's the thanks I get. When you pull them out of the gutter . . . (*He is completely hoarse with excitement; takes his hat from the table.*) Mna, I know your kind of woman well enough—well enough indeed . . .

ANNA *stands resolutely before him at the window, angry, resplendent in the light of the winter sunset. Suddenly the door opens, and, without seeing Max, who is still standing at the table, Toni (six years old, blond, lighthearted) comes running in. He throws his books on the chair by the door and runs toward Anna.*

TONI (*jubilant*): Mother!

ANNA *embraces and kisses him fervently.*

TONI (*going on quickly*): Mommy, Fritz saw the Christchild today already. Really, he did! And the teacher said that it flies through town every night. Is that true?

ANNA *lifts her face full of happiness toward Max, who is still hesitating at the door.*

TONI *since he doesn't get an answer, he follows the gaze of his mother and, surprised, looks back and forth from Max to Anna.*

ANNA *steps over to the alcove.*

TONI (*noticing this*): Don't, don't sew again right away, Mommy. (*Then playing up to Max*) Mister, are you the doctor? (*Takes his mother's hand.*) See how sore Mommy's hands are from sewing! (*To Anna*) Do they hurt?!

ANNA *smiles through her tears and kneels down, moved with love, to kiss the little child.*

*Curtain*

# Vigils
## A NIGHT PIECE

### A Play in One Act

*Adapted by Rainer Maria Rilke*
*from an idea by Fr. W. von Oestéren*

Characters:

FRITZ
JULIUS        } *Students, nineteen–*
MAX           *twenty-two years old*

MARIE
KATHY         } *Their girl friends*
BERTHA

ANNA, *the maid*
*Fritz's mother*

*Fritz is the youngest of the crowd. Blond, gangling. Marie is pale and wears her dark brown hair parted in the center. She has the large, deep eyes of a child. The others, according to their characters: Julius wears his hair short. In his features a certain inconsiderateness and harshness. Kathy: Typical of the refreshing, cheerful "little girl," etc. The mother is a shriveled-up old woman. Her presence must be felt rather than seen in the armchair. Although the stage is lighted only for a moment and then only partially and sparsely, all these hints must be scrupulously observed. It is natural that after the lamp is brought in, the stage*

83

*is illuminated only by it and by neither overhead nor footlights. Since the entire play is a single, large ensemble, all of the roles (except Anna, the maid) are equally important and part of the action.*

*The set is a plain, simple room—the residence of the student Fritz. Accordingly, the furniture is well used and practical. To be specific: An oval table covered by a cloth. The sofa possibly covered in a flowered material, chairs of a most ordinary sort, curved wood with woven cane.*

*On the desk (to the left): cigar boxes, photographs, books, and pamphlets. In addition: an old-fashioned, Empire-style bookcase, half covered in green material. Toward the back (according to your sensibility!) a bed or couch for sleeping. A small stove with flue in the corner.*

*Of importance is the armchair with a wide, projecting headrest that wraps around one's ears. It is covered with faded green rep fabric, and its back is half turned toward the audience. Plain lace curtains at the window. Both doors are single panels—not French doors. Scrubbed floors. The walls are in a gray-green pattern, preferably striped. Hanging on the walls: Above the sofa a large oval mirror in a gold frame. On both sides of the mirror are pictures of the family in the same kind of frame. The rest as you wish. The entryway opens onto the landing. The stairs are made of wood. The lamp which Anna brings in is an ordinary study lamp with a pyramid-shaped, milk-glass shade.*

*The play begins shortly before midnight. The time span of the play coincides exactly throughout with the actual passage of time and lasts around twenty to twenty-five minutes. The curtain rises slowly. The stage is dark. No footlights! The light of a moonless, clear, early autumn night encompasses the scene. Thus, the objects are seen in outline. Especially the armchair. After the curtain rises, the stage remains empty for a minute; as much time as it takes for everyone's eyes to get used to the dark. Then we hear a heavy door slam and lock on the ground floor. After around six seconds, we hear distant steps, both heavy and light;*

*then laughter and confused, incomprehensible talking. Nearer and nearer, louder and louder. Then distinct shouts like: "Oh my! Slow down!" And in between: "Shh! Shh!" And repeatedly, muffled laughter and giggling.*

## Scene One

*In front of the door: Fritz, Julius, Max, Marie (Mitzi), Kathy, Bertha.*

MAX: Oh, here already?

KATHY *(almost together)* } Dear God, I'm completely out of breath.

BERTHA } Maybe you'd like to keep climbing?

JULIUS: Come on now, hurry, open up—Fritz!

FRITZ: Alright, alright—where did I put that . . . Uh . . .

BERTHA *(in a shrill voice)*: Oh no! Max! I'm going to fall right back down the stairs!

JULIUS: Don't make so much noise.

MITZI: Fritz, can't you open the door?

FRITZ *(still trying the key)*: Sure, God knows what's wrong with . . .

MAX: Bertha, come here.

BERTHA *(threatening him jokingly)*: You!

JULIUS *(to Fritz, impatiently)*: Come on, let me have it, please.

KATHY: What's wrong with Fritz today?

JULIUS *(laughing irritably)*: There now. It wasn't even locked. You could have kept right on turning for quite some time, my friend.

*General laughter. The whole laughing confusion swirls through the hastily opened door and babbles unintelligibly in.*

## Scene Two

FRITZ (finally): It was open?!

KATHY: Open! Isn't that terrible? What if someone sneaked in and stole Fritz's treasures . . . *(Laughs)*

JULIUS: That would really be something. He'd probably bring everything back and add something to it—out of sympathy!

*Laughter. Max and Bertha are playing meanwhile behind the tablecloth. In doing so, Max bumps hard into Julius.*

JULIUS (*turns around*): What the . . . !

BERTHA *laughs in that bright, breathless, childlike laugh.*

MAX (*catches up to her near the window and kisses her*): Well, now who's stronger? (*Giggling*)

JULIUS (*sits down; acting superior*): Children!

KATHY: Well, it was nice of Fritz to bring us all up with him. Who'd want to go to sleep now anyway. Wait, Jule, I'll sit by you.

FRITZ: Alright now! Good Lord, what can I serve? Mitzi, you know, over there in the desk, I think, do we have a little bit of schnaps left?

MAX: Bravo!

FRITZ: And something to nibble on, too.

MITZI: Yes, but—light . . .

JULIUS (*stretching*): Well—I should think so!

MAX AND BERTHA (*almost together*): N-no . . . It's much nicer this way!

JULIUS: Of course! Like two pussycats.

FRITZ: Julius—do you have? . . .

JULIUS: Wait! (*Looks*)


## Scene Three

KATHY (*softly*): Fritz, what's that smell?

JULIUS (*without hearing the question*): I'm sure I left my lighter at the restaurant. Damn it all. Why didn't you remind me, Kathy? Who's got some matches?

FRITZ: Aren't there any on the desk?

MITZI: I'm looking . . . No.

KATHY (*to Julius, pointing at Max and Bertha*): *They* don't hear a thing!

JULIUS (*shouting*): Who's got some matches?—Max!—Are you deaf?

MAX: You want some matches? Well, why didn't you say so?— There you are!

*The sound of the matchbox landing on the tabletop is heard. They all grab for it.*

FRITZ (*seizes it*): Let me . . . Where's the candle?

MITZI (*approaching*): Here, I'll hold it for you.

*They are standing between the table and the desk, somewhat more toward the center.*

FRITZ: Well, there certainly aren't very many matches in here.

*With a vigorous effort, Fritz quickly and vigorously strikes a match a few times.—Finally we hear it break.*

MAX: Bravo, that's the way . . . you've got the idea.

BERTHA *laughs.*

KATHY: Don't you smell something, Jule?

JULIUS: No . . . just sulfur!

FRITZ (*already striking the third match*): Well, if it doesn't light pretty soon!

JULIUS (*ironically*): What slaves you are! One should just say: Let there be light. I just can't stand it. Such ineptitude. Hand them over!

KATHY: Oh—stay here, Jule. You know, I've been wanting to ask you if it's true, what Betty was saying . . . (*Whispering*)

BERTHA: But something really smells in here, don't you think so?

MAX (*inhaling*): Cheese.—Ah, apparently we're going to get some cheese to nibble on!

*Laughter.*

FRITZ (*nervously*): Now if this one doesn't . . . (*He quickly strikes a match; it flares up suddenly, flickers increasingly in all directions for five seconds, so that the room is slightly illuminated. Mitzi holds the candle up to it. The flame is snuffed out by the abrupt contact with the wick. He stamps his foot*): That was the last one!

### Scene Four

JULIUS: You really did it.

MITZI: You did it too quickly . . . Fritz . . .

FRITZ (*sullenly*): Oh—leave me alone.

MAX (*begins to sing*): "Bottle of wine, fruit of the vine . . ."

(*Laughter*)

MITZI (*softly*): Fritz, please tell me what's wrong.

FRITZ: Oh, I . . .

MITZI: Go on . . .

FRITZ: It's nothing.

MITZI: Since day before yesterday . . .

JULIUS: What's wrong with you two?

KATHY: Are you quarreling again?

MITZI (*artlessly*): I was just asking him to tell me what's wrong. He's been so . . .

KATHY: First he can't unlock the door; then he can't even light a candle.

MAX: That's like the story of the farmer's family that couldn't blow out a candle. Because their mouths were all crooked!— Want me to tell it to you, the whole story?

JULIUS (*pityingly*): Stop—please!

BERTHA: Tell *me*. Alright?

MAX: What? You haven't heard it? (*Laughs.*) That's good. Well, the farmer comes up and—goes ppff!

*Laughter, whispering.*

JULIUS (*to Fritz*): Don't torture the girl, be honest. Fritz! It's not fair this way.

MITZI: *Tell* me!

FRITZ: But you already know.

JULIUS: What?

KATHY (*from the sofa*): Leave him alone.

MITZI: About your mother—is that it?

FRITZ: She should have gotten here the day before yesterday. Something must have happened!

MITZI: Oh—really now . . .

JULIUS: Christ, what a sissy! He always thinks something must have happened!

FRITZ: Well, she's an old woman—and the trip . . .

MITZI: Just four hours!

JULIUS (*sighs impatiently; back at the table*): Kathy, please tell me something.—(*They whisper.*)

FRITZ: And she hasn't been very well either . . .

MITZI: Don't worry, Fritz. I'm sure she's alright. (*She embraces him. They kiss.*)

## Scene Five

FRITZ: You're right, Mitzi! (*Cheered up*)
*Bertha has been sitting on Max's lap so far. Now she jumps up and can hardly control her laughter.*
FRITZ (*coming over*): Shhh! Children! I'm going to go in the kitchen now; get some matches and light the lamp—and then Mitzi'll get the schnaps—alright?—and we'll have a good time.
JULIUS: Well, finally, Fredericus.

| | | |
|---|---|---|
| KATHY | | Great! |
| MAX | (*almost together*) | Bravo! |
| BERTHA | | Bravo! |

JULIUS *turns toward the door to the kitchen.*
MITZI: You won't find anything out there. You don't know where things are. Let *me*!
FRITZ: Yes, if you would, Mitzi . . . Or . . . did it just occur to you that the maid is out there. We could do things up in a grand style.
MITZI: Just wake her up?—
FRITZ: Yes, my dear. It won't hurt her. Besides, she left the door open today: the punishment must be carried out! (*Calls*) Anna!
KATHY: He's waking up the whole house.
JULIUS: She's not moving.
MAX: Want us to help you?
KATHY: Forward!
FRITZ: Quickly now: One . . . (*Giggling*) Two . . .
BERTHA *claps her hands.*
FRITZ:
MAX:
JULIUS (*all together*): . . . Three! . . .
KATHY:
BERTHA:
EVERYONE: Aaaa—nnaa!
*Giggling, three seconds.*
MAX: Shh!
*Everyone listens.*
ANNA (*in the kitchen. Stretches; we hear the bed creak, a sudden*

*movement, a long, inarticulate yawn, a few short, incomprehensible words . . . then):* Ye-es!?

MAX: Lord, she's in bad shape!

JULIUS: Well, I'd like to see what you'd do if you were blasted out of bed like that!

KATHY (*gaily*): Something's burning!

BERTHA: Fire!

MAX (*we sense that he is pointing to his heart when he says melodramatically*): Here!

*Fritz and Mitzi are standing by the kitchen door.*

FRITZ (*opens the door a crack*): Light, Anna; the lamp, quickly! —Alright?!

ANNA *incomprehensible mumbling.*

MITZI: Anna, did you hear?

ANNA (*sleepily*): Just a minute . . .

*We hear yawns, the bed creaking.*

FRITZ *shuts the door.*


## Scene Six

BERTHA (*anxiously*): Is the light coming?

MAX: Why all of a sudden?

BERTHA: I don't know, I just . . .

MAX *laughs.*

FRITZ (*to the others*): It's coming. (*To Mitzi*) Alright, dear, and now, go find the schnaps and set it out.—You like it, too, don't you? Yes, I know my little pussycat.

JULIUS: You're crazy, Kathy.

KATHY: Just be careful!

JULIUS: Nonsense.—Who has a good nose?

FRITZ (*laughs*): For what? (*He comes over to the table with Mitzi.*)

KATHY: It's—as if . . .

JULIUS (*pointing at Kathy*): She's been smelling God knows what all day.

KATHY: . . . like something scorched.

BERTHA (*suddenly joining in*): Yes—or—something rotten.

FRITZ (*to Mitzi*): Do you smell something, dear?

*Mitzi takes a few steps toward the center—the others whisper.*

FRITZ: Now?

MITZI: Lavender.

FRITZ *sniffs too now.*

MITZI: And yet—something else . . .

FRITZ: Yes, it is something like lavender.—That makes me think about mother again. She likes it so much . . .

MITZI (*trying to distract him*): Oh no, Fritz. It was our imagination. Lavender doesn't smell like that. Wait, Fritz, surely your mother will come tomorrow, and then you'll see what lavender's really like . . .

*Loud laughter at the table.*

JULIUS (*shouts*): Fritz!

KATHY: Fritz!

*Fritz and Mitzi join the others.*

KATHY (*giggling*): You really missed something! Those two over there . . . (*Points at Max and Bertha and titters.*)

JULIUS: Ah, sweet pleasures of my youth . . .
      I am too old to see your truth . . .

KATHY (*provoked*): Oh no!

MAX: What we're doing is none of your business. You can all go —stand on your heads—as far as I'm concerned.

BERTHA (*pouting*): That goes for me, too!

KATHY: Ah—look at Bertha there, that little Miss Perfect!

JULIUS: That's the worst kind!

*Meanwhile Mitzi has taken a brownish-green bottle and three glasses, each one different from the other, out of the bottom drawer of the desk; she brings these over to the table without any saucers.*

### Scene Seven

MITZI: But we've only got three glasses.

JULIUS: So much the better!

KATHY: Don't make a big thing out of it. Please. We can all drink out of the same glass.

FRITZ (*pours*): There's just enough light to pour.

MAX: Well, you missed here anyway.

FRITZ: Lap it up!
BERTHA (*giggling*): None for me, Fritz! } (*together*)
MAX (*melodramatically*): Careful with the precious spirits!
JULIUS: Comedian!
KATHY: Actually, he wanted to go into drama! Isn't that right, Maestro Max, you wanted to go into drama?
MAX: That's right, that's right.
JULIUS: Well, you would have gone a long way. You know what part you could have played? The balcony in *Romeo and Juliet*.
*Several giggles.*
MAX: Go ahead, laugh. If my parents had given me permission when I was a boy . . .
FRITZ: By the way, Max and Kathy, haven't I noticed that you don't call each other by your first names?!
KATHY: Yes—this gentleman . . .
FRITZ: You really should be more friendly. Let's drink to that!
MAX: Hmm! With schnaps? Well, then the friendship will snap easily.
KATHY: Then you, sir, will be the snapper, Mr. Max!
*Laughter.*
BERTHA: No—Max, no, not for anything—I'll get drunk!
MAX: Just a drop.
BERTHA: I get drunk in no time.
MAX: Then I'll carry you home.
BERTHA: Yes—and Lord knows what . . .
JULIUS: Why always think the worst right away!
FRITZ (*pointing at Kathy and Max*): First these two.
*Kathy and Max drink to friendship.*
MAX: Bottoms up!
KATHY: Bottoms up!
MAX: Ahem?!
KATHY: Now what?
MAX: A kiss?!
BERTHA (*blurts out, reproachfully*): Max!
JULIUS: Aha! Henpecked already.
KATHY: You wouldn't get one otherwise, Max, but since the little pussycat is showing her claws—there!—
*Kathy and Max give each other a noisy kiss.*

## Scene Eight

*Loud laughter and confusion for 15 to 20 seconds. Finally Bertha participates in it too, when Max plays up to her.*

MAX (*suddenly*): No really . . . Seriously.

*Laughter.*

MAX (*as before*): Be quiet now—and smell!

*These words sound serious and forceful. Everything is quiet. We hear the ticking of a clock in the room and somewhere the muffled striking of a tower clock. It remains quiet for five seconds. Then Kathy begins to titter softly. Everyone bursts out in howling laughter.*

JULIUS: That was another brilliant statement!

KATHY (*half suffocated with laughter*): Be quiet and—smell.

*Renewed laughter.*

JULIUS: This is really stupid!

FRITZ: Well, he's a jolly good fellow!

MITZI: For he's a jolly good fellow!

FRITZ: For he's a jolly good fellow!

EVERYONE: For he's a jolly good fellow,
      which nobody can deny!
      Hip, hip—hurray!

*Loud laughter, clinking of glasses, and confusion. Anna, a strong, flaxen-blond maid, enters barefoot, wearing a slip under her housecoat. She gropes forward in the dark, her eyes blinking and avoiding the light of the lamp which she carries at her left side. She walks phlegmatically toward the continuing laughter and up to the table. Julius moves over to Kathy, and she puts the lamp down.*

MAX (*shouts in the middle of laughter*): Have a good night's sleep!?

*Everyone is blinded—and can't stop laughing. Anna turns around, her steps dragging, and moves in the direction of the door. Suddenly she stops. She trembles all over and points with her right arm outstretched toward the armchair.*

ANNA: Oh, God in heaven! There's someone—there! (*She takes a step closer, covers her face with her hands, and howls*): Dead!

*At the first outcry, Fritz, Mitzi, and Julius jump up from the table.
Now everyone is struck dumb. Kathy's laughter is the last to die
out. Everyone follows the outstretched hand with blinded eyes.
In everyone's face, an expression of uncomprehending, obvious
shock and hollow fear.*

## Scene Nine

*Bertha hides her head on Max's chest. Max is trembling. Kathy
flees behind Julius. Mitzi glances fearfully up at Fritz with a look
of questioning fright. All the color is gone from Fritz's distorted
face. He stares at the armchair (four seconds), his neck stretched
out, his eyes feverish and glazed. He tries to move forward. He
staggers. He reaches with his left hand toward his throat, his right
hand flutters in the air, and he rasps tonelessly . . .*

FRITZ: Mother!

*Near to losing consciousness, he tries to hold on to the table,
knocks over the lamp, which immediately goes out.*

> *Deep darkness. A heavy fall.*
> *The curtain falls slowly.*

# Not Present

*A Play in Two Acts*

*Characters:*

MRS. GERTH
SOPHIE, *her daughter, recently married*
ERNST ERBEN, *Sophie's husband, an engineer*

*Setting: A country house in the vicinity of a medium-large city.
A bright, friendly living room, whose windows and alcove door
(the windows are tall and bright) look out into the garden where
it's spring. All the furniture is fairly new, arranged somewhat
clumsily and schematically, and definitely shows the desire and
opinion of the interior decorator, as is customary in the homes
of newlyweds. Everything is waiting to be used. The arrangement
is as follows: in the alcove, one wall of which is taken up by the
garden door, are flowers. The alcove is separated from the rest
of the room by a curtain draped in a conventional fashion. Similar
curtains hang in front of the tall windows and on both doors
(right and left), and the covers of the armchairs by the chimney
and around the salon table are of a corresponding pattern. The
couch, unusually wide, protrudes far into the room and is covered
with a rug. Pictures, inexpensive and not very numerous, are
placed about the room.*

# ACT ONE

## *Scene One*

### *Mrs. Gerth (the mother), Sophie*

MOTHER: I keep wanting to walk through the whole house. Darling, you've really done well. When I think about our floors in the old houses, there on Spornergasse. You know: when you come downstairs, it's like crawling out of the chimney. But here? You could eat off the floors, not a speck of dust . . . (*She interrupts herself suddenly.*) But I meant to ask you, Sophie. Do you really like that there? (*She points at the couch.*) I just can't get around it. It's in my way everywhere I go. The way I bickered with the decorator. But he kept insisting that something like that had to be at an angle. I can't bear to look at it.

SOPHIE: Lord, it's not as bad as all that. It doesn't have to stick out this far, and as soon as everything else is in order, we can take another look at it. For now I'll leave it the way it is.

MOTHER: Just think, child, he wanted to put the desk the same way; diagonally across the room. "My good man," I said to him, "are you . . ." Well, obviously he was a bit . . . (*Makes a gesture to her forehead.*) After all, a desk goes against the wall.

SOPHIE: I guess he thought of that because of the light.

MOTHER: Right; that's the stupid excuse he had. No light that way. What do you need light for? You won't sit there twice all year.

SOPHIE (*in playful horror*): But Mother . . .

MOTHER: Now don't act that way to me—oh, I almost called you "Miss"—what an insult. Anyone can see that you should be addressed as "Ma'am." You're properly mature and grown-up now.

SOPHIE (*nestles up to her mother*): I'm so happy.

MOTHER: That's understandable. And that's why I'm saying: you won't be spending much time sitting over there by that thing, since you'll be able to talk to your Mister Ernst like—this (*forms her mouth into a kiss*) anytime you want to. Right?

Before, I guess those secret love notes back and forth were all
that mattered. Then the desk was more important than the
bed. Hm?

SOPHIE *says nothing in her embarrassment.*

MOTHER: Well, now that struggle's all over, and you two have
gone through with it. Now we can talk about it. I knew about
it for a long time and kept a tight hold on your papa.

SOPHIE (*hesitatingly*): I've always wanted to ask you: why did
papa dislike Ernst for such a long time?

MOTHER: Lord, that's just his way. You know him as well as I
do. By the way, he always liked Ernst.

SOPHIE: But? . . .

MOTHER: Those relatives in Vienna didn't seem quite right to
him.

SOPHIE *looks up inquisitively.*

MOTHER (*apologetically*): They're honest and respectable people,
I'm sure, although they're not very educated. And that's what
bothers papa. You know how he is. (*Breaking off quickly*) But
that makes it all the more wonderful about Ernst, the way he
worked his way up. Right? He was always at the top of his
class, and now he's the best man at the factory. Everyone likes
him. He has a good career ahead of him . . . but—here I go,
telling you about the virtues of your one and only Ernst. As if
you didn't know all that best of all!

SOPHIE (*with childlike pride*): He really is wonderful!

MOTHER (*laughing*): Yes, yes—I know.—Well, I'd better be
going now, child. If I stay around to hear the end of the list
of his virtues, they'll starve to death at home: papa and Agla.
Of course, Agla never thinks of food. But papa has to have
his supper on the table punctually at eight, and I haven't laid
anything out for the cook.—(*Dogmatically*) You should keep
that in mind, too. Punctuality. That's the main thing. Dinner's
at one o'clock: punctually at one the soup must be on the table.
Supper's at eight—and the same thing with breakfast . . . Well,
I've told you all this already ten thousand times . . . You're
probably thinking, that old pedant of a mother. But—that's the
way it has to be. When there isn't any order, the money just
rolls away twice as fast . . . (*Prepares to leave.*)

SOPHIE: No, wait a little while. Ernst should be here any minute. He promised to be back at five, and Ernst is (*with special teasing emphasis*) also very "punctual."

MOTHER: Well, I'd certainly like to see that. All right, I'll wait a few minutes. (*She sits down on the edge of the couch, Sophie next to her.*) You never know how or where to sit down on a contraption like this. (*Looking around*) But anyway: it's lovely here—so bright and comfortable. And that you have the little garden, too . . . That's a thousand times better than a honeymoon trip, isn't it?

SOPHIE *nods.*

MOTHER: Would you have rather gone away?

SOPHIE: Well, you know—Venice. Yes. When I heard that Ernst couldn't get any time off now, it really made me sad for a while. But only for a while. At that time I still thought we'd have to live in the city. You really surprised us with all this.

MOTHER: You won't miss anything. You can go down there later, to Italy. You romantic dreamers. The pigeons on St. Mark's Square won't have starved to death by then.

SOPHIE: Oh, I'm so content here now. It's so lovely, and it's all ours. Ernst says the same thing, too: once we get settled in.

MOTHER: Well, for me that would mean putting sofas right up against the wall where they belong. (*They laugh.*)

## Scene Two

### Same characters, plus Ernst Erben

*Ernst and Sophie embrace. In the meantime, the clock begins to strike five. Sophie releases herself from her husband's arms.*

SOPHIE (*drolly*): Shhh!

MOTHER *and* ERNST: What's going on?

SOPHIE: I want you to hear, Mama. Right on the last stroke of five. And here I have the honor of presenting to you my punctual husband.

ERNST: What are you talking about?

MOTHER (*offering Ernst her hand*): Good evening, my dear Ernst. A new leaf in your laurel wreath: your punctuality.

SOPHIE: Now you've won mama over completely.

ERNST: How is that?

MOTHER: Well, my dear son-in-law, I have discovered many good traits in you, such as that you don't smoke, etc. But now that I know that you're punctual, too—I tell you: you can wrap me right around your little finger.

ERNST: Well, that's not an accomplishment; that's an old habit.

MOTHER: And anyway (*jokingly*) what does the approval of your mother-in-law matter? Besides, she only pops in whenever the whim strikes her, at any time of the day or night . . .

ERNST: You don't believe that yourself, Mama; you know how much we have to thank you for.

MOTHER: Oh, thanks for what. No one's thankful when he's happy, and that's the way it should be. Yes, yes. But I really must apologize for stopping by so soon again.

SOPHIE (*reproachfully*): Mama.

MOTHER: Not to you, to your husband. And better than any apology would be if I pack myself up and go now.

ERNST: You mustn't take away our peace and quiet by leaving, and you'll take it amiss, too, if you go just when I come in.

SOPHIE (*pushes her gently back onto the couch*): There.

ERNST (*gets an armchair and sits down in front of the two women*): How are things with my father-in-law?

MOTHER: As always: fine, except for his temper and his arthritis. It bothers him more now in the spring, and he becomes quite helpless when he's in pain. On top of that, he doesn't know what to do with himself now that he's not going to the office anymore. And I can't always tell him a funny story either, something that will bring him out of it and humor him, and well . . . we're just a pair of old shoes.

ERNST: I'm not a bit worried about that. Anyone who's as busy as you are, Mama, won't have time to wear out. And after all, that's the main thing: not to wear out.

MOTHER: That may happen sooner than you think. I'm just not comfortable anymore inside my four walls since I've seen everything over here. And then there's also the business with Agla.

ERNST *gets up and goes over to the window.*

SOPHIE: What's the matter with her now?

MOTHER: The same old story. I don't understand it: she lies around with her books all day, or she runs around in the streets. I don't know why. Either she doesn't say anything at all, or she says something in a way that I can't understand. I keep asking myself: is what she says so clever, or is it all nonsense?

SOPHIE: Oh, it's all nonsense.

MOTHER: But you haven't heard anything yet. You ought to hear her *now*. Ever since you got married. It's been awful since then. Until it got to be too much for papa, and he's always been very lenient with her. And just imagine, I have to tell you about this: Recently I said to him that he ought to talk to the child; forcefully, I said. When I came back two hours later, there sat the old man, there he sat with his eyes shining, listening while Agla spoke. As extravagantly as ever. I think she even gave him some sort of advice. I don't know, there's something about that girl—when I look at you and me—Sophie—I can't believe she's my daughter. You're so level-headed, such a home-body . . .

ERNST (*carelessly, from the window*): Perhaps you shouldn't let her run around so much by herself?

MOTHER: You tell her that. She wants to be independent.

SOPHIE: Rubbish, I was independent, too, you know, and the looks I would have gotten from you if I'd acted that way.

MOTHER: So I go to her and I say: Agla, that's not proper. All well and good. She locks herself up in her room and stays there, quite obediently, until I beg her to go out again. The way she looks. She'll be eighteen soon and she's still so delicate. She has to get some air.—Since she doesn't want to go anywhere else. I could have presented her a long time ago. At that time we still had social connections. All your dance partners would have been interested in your sister. That's all gone now. Oh, it worries me so much.

SOPHIE (*seriously*): Just tell her I think she's being a child, that —she'll know what I mean.

MOTHER: But she really looks so miserable right now, that I scarcely dare tell her anything.—On top of that, there's also the city air. I've thought to myself, now, when the sun does such wonders, maybe two or three days, of course only two or three days, out somewhere . . .

ERNST (*turning around*): Yes—yes (*quickly*) perhaps that would be best.

MOTHER: It couldn't be for any longer—but could she, so she · wouldn't be among strangers, sit out in your garden for two or three days? . . .

SOPHIE (*hastily*): No.

ERNST (*likewise*): No.

*Sophie and Ernst exchange an involuntary glance of amazement. The mother looks at them, confused by the decisiveness of their tone.*

ERNST (*approaching with some embarrassment*): I mean— around here—we don't yet have—

SOPHIE: Ernst means—our home—

MOTHER (*has gotten hold of herself, laughing*): Well, I really am something. I'm no good for anything anymore. To suggest guests to young newlyweds. Yes, and such a crazy guest. And in the first week of their honeymoon.—(*Laughing*) Just look, dear, I honestly believe your husband's blushing for you. Hm? or are you blushing yourself, too—right! You, too! Well, aren't you sweet. They're both blushing. (*She caresses Sophie.*) Now, now—this clumsy, old mother-in-law. Thinking that two or three days would be a small sacrifice. Two or three days!—an eternity. Well, that's what happens: I become young again when I'm with you children. And so completely young that I am quite naive.—But don't you start blushing all over again. Lord, Lord. I'd better leave this minute. Heaven knows what havoc I'll wreak otherwise. Listen (*takes Ernst gently by the arm*) her face is all red. See that you wash it off . . . See to it . . . (*She kisses Sophie quickly, winks at Ernst, and goes to the door. To Ernst, who is about to accompany her*) Don't bother, I can find my own way out.—*Will you please* go to your little wife! (*Laughs. Exits.*)

### Scene Three

### Sophie, Ernst

SOPHIE *stands pensively, somewhat embarrassed.*

ERNST (*approaches her*): Mama's right. Now first give me a nice kiss.

SOPHIE (*relieved. Kisses him*): Yes.

ERNST: Don't I get any more?

SOPHIE: Oh yes, as many as you want. Do you really love me?

ERNST: Of course. That's something we've never talked about. (*Kisses her on the forehead.*) Has my little wife been working hard?

SOPHIE: And how. It's such a pleasure keeping myself busy with all these things. Come, I have to show you the kitchen. Everything is new and clean as a whistle. (*To Ernst, who is making a move in that direction*) No, not yet; for that festive occasion everything will have to be completely ready first. I'm not quite finished yet. You can't look at the kitchen until it's just as shiny as your office is dusty. Tell me, does it have to be like that?

ERNST: You forget, child, that in our office there aren't any lovely hands like yours, just a couple of lazy janitors who aren't even allowed to touch anything lying on the tables.

SOPHIE: I see, they aren't allowed to touch anything. Hm. That's how secret your affairs are there. You know, if it wouldn't embarrass you, why don't you take me along to that drab office of yours and tell me that (*she takes him by the arm*) that needs to go there, and that over there, and that thing you can't see under all that dust, right there . . .

ERNST: You little schemer.

SOPHIE: No, I'm completely serious. Then I'd clean things up for you. It's not just that. That's not the only reason. You could get sick from breathing in all that stuff day after day. You already look quite yellow to me!

ERNST: Really? A few minutes ago someone told me just the opposite.

SOPHIE: He certainly doesn't know what he's talking about.

ERNST: Oh, I'm sure he does, since he's someone that you say understands everything.

SOPHIE: Oh, come on . . .

ERNST: Well?

SOPHIE: You mean the reverend?

ERNST: Exactly. I'm getting jealous of your old teacher.

SOPHIE (*playing it up*): Hmmm! You really should be a little jealous of *him*. I'm sure that won't hurt you. If the reverend were about forty years younger, and if he weren't a reverend and if you weren't on this earth—I'm sure I would have married him. Well—it didn't miss by much, did it?

ERNST: No.—A mere trifle, which we might still be able to correct. For that reason I've asked him to come over sometime soon. I wanted to bring him along just now.

SOPHIE (*sincerely*): Too bad—

ERNST: He was just on his way into town; he had something to do there—also wanted to see your parents.

SOPHIE: That's sweet. Mama will arrive at the house the same time he does. Oh, I completely forgot, would you like some tea—Ernst?

ERNST (*breaking away from his thoughts*): No, thanks . . . But we don't have any visitors other than the pastor, do we?

SOPHIE (*hesitatingly*): No, why do you ask?

ERNST (*casually*): It's best being alone, isn't it?

SOPHIE (*shyly*): Oh yes—I can, of course, ask the reverend not to come now . . .

ERNST: No, no, child, I just mean . . . I just meant strangers . . . just . . .

SOPHIE (*uneasily*): I see.

## Scene Four

### The same characters

*Ernst sits down on the couch; Sophie paces back and forth for a moment, hiding her impatience poorly.*

SOPHIE (*stops in front of Ernst*): I have to ask you something.

ERNST (*seemingly composed*): Well?!—

SOPHIE: A while ago, when my mother suggested that my sister—
come out and stay with us—(*She hesitates.*)

ERNST: Yes—(*aggravated*)—well, what about it?—

SOPHIE: Are you angry?

ERNST (*laughing forcibly*): Now why don't you tell me quickly
what's bothering you?

SOPHIE: As soon as mama suggested it, you said "No" so
strangely. So . . .

ERNST (*in an attempt to joke*): You silly girl. The things you
imagine. How can anyone say "no" strangely. You just say
"yes" or "no."—Well, in view of several circumstances which
I'd like to explain to you in greater detail (*he pulls her onto his
lap*) I allowed myself to choose the latter. You said exactly
the same thing, didn't you?

SOPHIE (*mechanically*): Yes, that's true—I said exactly the same
thing.

ERNST (*distracting her*): Well then. Now I've been absolved.
Hm? (*Kisses her.*)

SOPHIE (*resisting*): Don't.

ERNST: Now what?—

SOPHIE: I'm sorry, I was thinking. Now, give me a big kiss.

ERNST: Oh, child, can you be thinking, too? (*Kisses her.*)

SOPHIE (*during his kisses, shyly*): I've got something on my
mind, Ernst—I didn't want to tell you, but . . .

ERNST (*uneasy again*): It can't be as bad as all that.

SOPHIE: Maybe it's not so bad. I just can't make it out. (*She gets
up from his lap.*) You'll be able to understand what it means.
(*She stands before him, thinking.*)

ERNST (*says nothing. Struggles with a decision and then hands
Sophie a letter*): I think it might be best if you read this.

*Sophie takes the letter quickly, uncrumples it with trembling
fingers, and reads it in breathless suspense; suddenly, with intense hatred, she begins to tear it up into tiny scraps; then she
steps on the pieces that have fallen to the floor, as if they were on
fire—her face is completely distorted.*

ERNST (*astonished*): But child, child.

SOPHIE (*pushes his soothing arms away*): And you?

ERNST: Calm down, darling.—As you see—I was here at five.

SOPHIE (*slowly regaining her composure*): Yes, yes, you were here.

ERNST: Agla has often sent me letters like that.

SOPHIE: It's wicked, it's . . .

ERNST: It's sick.

SOPHIE: My own sister. (*All at once in sudden mistrust*): And you never, never went there, not even once?

ERNST: Never.

SOPHIE (*anxiously*): Never go there—promise me.

ERNST: I promise you. And now listen to me. We need to talk this over quietly. Sit down. (*They sit next to each other on the couch.*)

SOPHIE (*relieved*): And you really love me?

ERNST: Very much, Sophie. Now pay attention. All these crazy letters your sister sent me, I burned them, mostly without even reading them. That was wrong of me. We should have read them together and done something about them—together.

SOPHIE (*in intense agreement*): Yes.

ERNST: That way everything probably would have been settled by now. A woman can find the solution more easily. I don't understand things like this at all. I dread this kind of extravagant behavior. Such things are not worth thinking about, and yet they are a constant bother at work and elsewhere. Your sister is sick. Those are all words she doesn't even understand. Fantasies which, I'm sure, don't have anything to do with me— after all, she hardly knows me—but rather some kind of hero of her dreams. If I could speak to her just once, she would certainly get rid of her illusions right away—

SOPHIE *gestures.*

ERNST: But that wouldn't work now. It's gone too far. And that's why we should do it *this* way. We need to fight against this like two good friends. I mean: We need to be completely truthful with one another. Tell each other everything about this problem, without any exceptions. Do you want to?

SOPHIE: Yes, everything.—

ERNST: That way we'll see it through together. After all, you know your sister better than I do . . .

SOPHIE: I'm afraid of her.

ERNST: There's no reason for that. Look, if we tell each other everything—what harm can she do us?

SOPHIE: She's always seemed so mysteriously threatening to me.

ERNST: Oh, we'll be able to handle her.

SOPHIE (*anxiously*): And you don't think . . .

ERNST: What?

SOPHIE: That she'll . . .

ERNST *looks at her questioningly.*

SOPHIE (*confused*): That she'll do it anyway . . .

ERNST: What?

SOPHIE: What she said in the letter . . .

ERNST: No, you don't have to worry about that, Sophie. People don't drown themselves as quickly as that. It sounds very nice in writing and is quite appropriate as the final chapter of a novel. But to actually do it—without even saying . . .

SOPHIE (*startled*): Saying—she did.

ERNST: What?

SOPHIE: She told me.

*Ernst jumps up.*

SOPHIE: God, I've been wanting to tell you all this time. But it was so awful. Forgive me. I—(*She breaks into tears.*)

*Ernst paces back and forth in agitation.*

SOPHIE: I wish I'd told you immediately. But I always felt: I'd lose you—if I said anything.

ERNST (*harshly*): When was it?

*Sophie struggles with her tears. Ernst calms her impatiently.*

ERNST: We both want to be truthful now, don't we? Alright then.

SOPHIE: Yes. (*Pulls herself together.*) The night before the wedding. I was already in bed. That's when she came to me . . . (*Her voice falters from excitement.*)

ERNST: None of this is your fault; be sensible.

SOPHIE (*with difficulty*): She came to me and said: ". . . You . . . you mustn't marry him . . . I'm in love with him . . . he belongs to me . . ."

ERNST (*stops*): He—belongs to me?

SOPHIE: At first I laughed; after all, I knew . . . But Agla was so frightening. Her eyes were huge in the dark, and completely wild. I became terribly afraid. "He must belong to me," she said.

ERNST (*shakes his head*): And you?

SOPHIE: Me? I don't know anymore. That I'd tell mother—that we'd promised each other, that you cared for me . . . that you liked me very much—loved me . . . and then—(*Standing before her, Ernst softly strokes her hair.*) Then she went away. And at the door, she said, in an entirely different voice—really strangely: "Then I'm going to—then I'm going to . . ." (*She clings fearfully to Ernst.*) I can still hear it.—That's all she said. But I felt: she'll do it—she'll do it. She'll kill herself. Oh, what a night. I couldn't shake loose the idea: something had happened to you. I wanted to go to you. I prayed till morning. I prayed so much. And I still didn't feel any better. Not until I saw you that morning—happy and unharmed . . . (*She embraces him passionately.*)

ERNST (*pensively*): Is that everything?

SOPHIE (*relieved*): Everything . . . And now it's off my chest. It was still bothering me. Now I'll be happy again, the way I was that morning. (*She embraces him again.*)

ERNST: You poor thing.

SOPHIE: Oh, don't think about it anymore. I'm so happy now that you know. So free.

ERNST: Yes—let's not talk about it anymore. Just that one thing: stand by each other and tell the truth.

SOPHIE (*gets up*): Yes.

ERNST: Complete honesty.

SOPHIE (*filled with joyful expectation*): Let's look deep into each other's hearts—alright?

ERNST (*moved, likewise happy again*): You darling!

SOPHIE: Sweetheart!

*They hold each other by the hand and look trustingly into each other's eyes.*

## Scene Five

### The same characters

ERNST: Shouldn't we light the lamp?

SOPHIE: But it's so nice like this.

ERNST: I've still got a little work to do.

SOPHIE: Rest a while longer. Look how pretty it is outside. When you look out like this, doesn't it seem as though our garden extends way, way out to the towers.

ERNST: You certainly get carried away.

SOPHIE: I'm just learning how. At home there was never enough quiet—but now. I wasn't mature enough, then, either.

ERNST: To get carried away?

SOPHIE: Yes, you have to be mature enough if it's really to be an art. First you have to love someone the way I love you.

ERNST (*warmly*): You're my golden angel!

SOPHIE: That's what I want to be. But not "golden"—please. I'd rather be—alive.

ERNST: Alright, my living angel then.

SOPHIE (*strokes his hair affectionately. Playfully*): But you sting. Your hair is so short. Get away from me!

ERNST (*laughing, takes a few steps back*): All of a sudden.

SOPHIE: There, you see, that's what you get now that I've learned to get carried away. Now I'd prefer you with long, golden locks. (*Laughs exuberantly.*) But Ernst, you used to write poems, too, didn't you? Now—you mustn't look at me so fiercely. I mean a long, long, time ago. When you were around seventeen?—

ERNST: Seventeen? I'll tell you, my child, exactly what I did when I was seventeen. Let's see: At that time I was in high school, and besides that I tutored lazy children, and at night—I probably copied some stuff for a few pennies as long as my eyes and the light held out. And if there still was a little bit of night left by then, I probably preferred sleeping—to writing poems. (*Embarrassed, Sophie says nothing.*) No, I never had time to be romantic. It's the same way as far as the long hair is concerned. When you have to get up early in the morning in bad light, you don't spend a lot of time in front of the mirror.—

It wasn't until you came along that I started being a little vain,
my child . . . (*Sophie remains standing there in thought.*) What
are you thinking about?

SOPHIE: I'm thinking about your copying at night.—But tell me
—you never—you never went hungry, did you?

ERNST: That, too.

*Sophie looks shyly at him in admiration.*

ERNST (*sincerely*): Well, I lived through it without any harm.
But you realize now that my time was limited. If I had acted
like most people, where would I be now? For me it meant
looking straight ahead, neither left nor right—all the time.
That's why I was so afraid of women, even you.

SOPHIE: Really?

ERNST: You were the first one I couldn't get out of my mind. Yes,
you silly thing, you bothered me terribly. I just had to find
time for you. But even *now* I don't have any time for getting
carried away. I see quite clearly where our garden ends.

SOPHIE (*drolly*): You poor thing, don't be sad on account of
that. It'll come to you sooner or later.

ERNST (*making a joke*): You don't say!

SOPHIE: It comes to everyone sometime.

ERNST (*curtly*): Well—I'm too old for that.—And now let's turn
on the light.

SOPHIE (*goes to the dressing table on which the lamp is sitting*):
Alright, be impatient, I'll let you get to your plans.

*Ernst sit down at the desk; Sophie puts the lighted lamp before
him, kisses him on the forehead, and exits to the right.*


### Scene Six

#### The same characters

*Ernst reads his plans. After a while he leans back, then gets up,
opens the mailbox in the alcove door, and takes out some newspaper and letters. He lays everything on the table. He scrutinizes
just one letter at the lamp, then hurls it aside with a soft curse,
and sits back down again. Pause.*

SOPHIE (*at the door to the right*): Was someone here?

ERNST: No.

SOPHIE (*coming in*): Would it bother you if I stayed here in the room?

ERNST: Oh, no.

*Sophie comes forward.*

ERNST: Oh—by the way, there's another one of those letters.

SOPHIE (*apprehensive, rushes to him*): Another one?

ERNST (*without looking at her*): Here—take a look at it. (*Holds the letter out to her.*)

SOPHIE (*hesitates for a while. Then she violently tears open the envelope and scans the letter, standing in the light of the lamp next to Ernst, who appears to be concentrating. Then she reads it again, and slowly yet a third time, with uncertainty slides it back in the envelope, and places her hand on Ernst's shoulder*): I think we won't have to struggle anymore.

ERNST (*without looking up, off-handedly*): Why is that?

SOPHIE (*lays the letter on the desk*): Read it.

ERNST (*angrily*): Child, I really don't have time.

SOPHIE (*with certainty*): It's the last one.

ERNST *looks up questioningly.*

SOPHIE: She did it today.

*Ernst forces a laugh and reads.*

SOPHIE: Totally different, isn't it? Totally calm?

ERNST (*puts the letter aside angrily*): Oh, now stop it. (*Pause.*)

SOPHIE (*coming forward*): I don't know, I'd like to go home for a moment, to my parents.

ERNST: Nonsense.

*Sophie sits down on the front edge of the couch. Pause.*

ERNST: I'm really getting hungry, child, aren't we going to eat supper soon?

SOPHIE (*without understanding, listening*): Shh.

ERNST (*looks around*): What's the matter?

SOPHIE: Someone's in the garden. I'm sure mama sent someone.

ERNST (*impatiently*): I don't hear anything.—You're really being childish.

SOPHIE (*with emphasis*): Shh!

ERNST (*gets up*): It's nothing.

SOPHIE (*firmly*): Just listen. Someone's trying to find the door. Please go and see. (*She stands up, listening.*)

ERNST (*shrugs his shoulders, gets the lighted lamp, and walks slowly toward the alcove door. He flings it open and takes a step outside, holding the lamp out into the dark*): Is someone there?

*Curtain*

# ACT TWO

*The living room still has the same stereotyped, sterile atmosphere as before. Lots of things on the tables and on the wardrobe, which has mirrors set in its doors. Clearly visible outside the windows: Autumn. A foggy day. Early in the morning.*

## Scene One

*The stage is set as in Act One. Mrs. Gerth is sitting near the front. Ernst is standing by the window near the desk.*

MOTHER: It was right of you, Ernst, to call the doctor. This way, at least, we have some idea of what's wrong. Strange. Sophie was always so healthy; I never would have thought that this would be so hard on her. But of course: when she gets over this, she'll just start blooming again. (*Ernst drums with his fingers on the window-pane.*) I suppose you have to go to the office soon?

ERNST (*looks at the clock*): Yes, in a moment.

MOTHER: It's really unfortunate you have such an extraordinary amount of work to do just now. And for weeks now. Will it last much longer?

ERNST (*turns around. Curtly*): Why?

MOTHER: You don't look well. It's no wonder. They've really burdened you with too much work.

ERNST: There are many things left over from summer.

MOTHER: I see. I just fear for the day when you'll get sick, too . . .

*Ernst wards off this remark with a gesture of annoyance.*

MOTHER (*stands up, goes to him, and puts her hand on his shoulder*): Look, Ernst, isn't it possible that you might be able to get a bit more time off—now—after all, you didn't take any vacation.

ERNST (*hesitating*): I really feel fine (*loudly, tormented*) and I have to work, work.—(*Looking up*) Really, Mama, I am *quite all right.*

MOTHER: It's not merely because of that. (*Ernst looks at her questioningly.*) It's also because, forgive me, I'm always quite frank—it's making Sophie feel so miserable. She's alone so much. (*Ernst shrugs his shoulders.*) She needs you twice as much just now. Your little wife wants to be sheltered and pampered. She worries about you. And she's alone all day and gets all kinds of thoughts in her head.

ERNST (*anxiously*): Do you think so?

MOTHER: Yes, she thinks about herself and broods too much. She worries about this and that and who knows what else. And then she always worries about you, whether everything in the house is the way you want it, and whether there isn't something you need. She would really like to look after everything, but she can't; and she knows she can't depend on the servants. It torments her. And since you don't show very much concern about her, she is forced to start feeling that you reproach her for not doing everything. *But she can't do any more.*

ERNST: But that's not the way it is at all.

MOTHER: She sees it that way and worries.—Look, winter is just around the corner.—If she has to face cold weather feeling this poorly.—(*Pause.*)

ERNST (*shuddering*): It's winter, yes (*as if involuntarily, he runs his hand wearily over his forehead*) and she died in the spring —in the middle of spring . . . (*Quickly*) But I've got to do my work—so much work.

MOTHER (*gently*): Forget that, Ernst. Don't think about it.

ERNST: Does he still talk about her often?

MOTHER: Father? He's still completely broken by it all.—I wanted to ask this of you, too—if you happen to visit us, don't speak with him about Agla; it still affects him too much. And don't think about it yourself, either. I hoped you'd forgotten about it long ago. (*Pause*)

ERNST (*goes over to the couch, sits down heavily, and holds his head in his hands*): Forgotten? What do I have to forget? I have hardly any memory of her at all. I hardly knew her. I hardly know what she looked like. I can only guess: was she blonde? Yes, more or less. Was she small, was she . . . ? I can only guess. I don't know. I just know that she died for me. (*He breaks into tears.*)

MOTHER (*alarmed, comes over to him*): For God's sake. What's wrong with you? You know that the unfortunate child was sick, that she was . . .

ERNST (*looks up and shakes his head*): I don't know *anything*.

MOTHER (*fearfully*): Sophie is in the next room. She mustn't suspect that you still think about Agla sometimes.

ERNST (*getting up*): Ah—that's why I must work. (*He gets ready to leave.*)

MOTHER (*calmly*): Listen to me a little longer, Ernst. You're such a sober and sensible person; you mustn't get carried away by such things.

ERNST: Yes. I have always felt so secure, so above things like that . . . But that's just the problem. You see, Mama, I have always understood everything in life. There were no miracles, not even any surprises. Everything was so clear. Everything was: work. Even my love, Sophie. I won her over quietly and carefully, step by step. And then along comes the one thing I *don't* understand. (*Loudly*) There is something I don't understand. I can't get over it. I don't believe in myself anymore. There's no way for me to believe in myself anymore. I have been proven wrong. I can start at the beginning.

MOTHER: You're under strain.

ERNST (*softly*): So to you this is nothing extraordinary. You think this sort of thing happens every day. It's not worth mentioning further. You happen to hear that so and so died for you. You hardly knew him. But that doesn't matter to you. Who was this person actually? How did this life appear that he should destroy it for your sake? What did it contain? You don't ask. It fits so completely into your experience. Someone holds out his life to you, like a white sheet of paper, and asks: write your name here. And if you don't feel like doing it—naturally, he tears the white sheet of paper—before your eyes—right down the middle. Oh, it's really so simple. God. (*With a sigh, he covers his face with his hands.*)

MOTHER: Shh!—Ernst, please! You're frightening me. (*Comes closer.*) Haven't we often talked about this calmly before? Everything was all right then. You're really over-strained now. Pull yourself together. You'll get over it.

ERNST: Yes, when I'm sitting at my desk. Or when I'm working somewhere on something in the factory, when I'm standing at the machine, and see how smooth and hard and certain everything turns out. It all goes away there. There I tell myself: that's life. There I can be myself again—but . . .

MOTHER: And if you'll listen to an old woman, I'll give you the best cure. Stay at home more. Sit down with Sophie. Read something out loud to her, tell her stories.

ERNST *makes an impatient gesture.*

MOTHER: Believe me. She loves you so much. She'll thank you for it. She doesn't suspect what's bothering you, and she must not suspect it. And that is why she will be able to remove it gently from your soul. Don't you ever think of the fact that she is bearing a life for you, that this is a blessed time . . .

ERNST *nods.*

MOTHER: Or do you want her to worry and get sick, very sick . . .

ERNST (*startled*): Did the doctor? . . .

MOTHER: She is so delicate.

ERNST (*pulling himself together*): I have to go now. (*Hesitating*) But—perhaps I'll be able to break away for a while and come back in an hour . . .

MOTHER (*breathing a sigh of relief*): I knew you would.

ERNST: Tell her.

MOTHER: I will. She'll be so pleased. (*Happily*) My strong and wonderful boy. People like us have survived all kinds of things, and yet we are not made of such healthy stock.

ERNST (*much moved, embraces her*): Mama!

MOTHER (*holding back her tears*): Now, now . . . go quickly, so Sophie won't have long to wait. You'll come back, won't you?

ERNST (*resolutely*): I promise.
*Leaves through the door in the alcove.*


### Scene Two

*Mrs. Gerth walks back and forth, putting the chairs in order and brushing off the tablecloth on the round table. Meanwhile, Sophie comes in from the right. She is wearing a white housecoat which flows loosely from her shoulders; she is very pale and apprehensive.*

SOPHIE (*startled*): My God, Mama, now you're even straightening up the house. Please let me do it.

MOTHER (*turning around*): Certainly not. Well, did our little wife have a good rest?

SOPHIE (*wearily*): Oh, as usual. (*She tries to brush off the tablecloth some more.*)

MOTHER: Well, I'm not surprised. Would you stop that, you silly little . . . Lie down on that weird sofa of yours this instant! You shouldn't have gotten up in the first place.

SOPHIE (*timidly*): Am I really that sick?

MOTHER: Our little mother is doing exactly as well as she should —but she doesn't take care of herself, getting up and around the house too much and trying to do too much, and so she would do better to stay in bed.

SOPHIE: Oh, please, anything but that. Don't ask me to stay in bed.

MOTHER: Well, that's not really necessary. I know you'd much rather be on your crazy couch. Wait a minute, I'll go and get you a pillow and a warm blanket.

SOPHIE *refuses.*

MOTHER: Don't argue with me. Our little wife is going to sit right here and look at the newspapers—(*gently pushes her onto one of the armchairs and puts a newspaper on the round table*) and wait till I come back and get her place ready; and then we'll put a comfortable chair right by that silly slanty couch—but I'm not going to tell you until I come back, who it's for.

SOPHIE *nods, smiling.*

MOTHER: But only if she's been really good. (*Kisses her daughter, exits to the right.*)

*Sophie sits there a while, without moving, in the same spot. Then she gets up, supporting herself with effort on the arm of one of the easy chairs, moves with groping steps to the front of the dressing table, straightens her hair, drops her hands helplessly, and walks over near the window. Outside the autumn park is visible. The storm is howling in the chimney. She looks out the window for a while, presses her handkerchief to her eyes, and cries softly. Pause.*

MOTHER (*comes through the door on the right with pillows and a blanket under her arm, looks first toward the easy chair in the foreground in which she had left her daughter. Surprised*) Well—is the little wife playing hide and seek? (*She tosses the pillows and blanket on the chair.*) I'll find her, I'll . . . (*Notices her daughter by the window; she comes forward to her mother with a feeble smile.*)

MOTHER: What do you think you're doing over there, so near the window! Right where the cold air comes in, such a careless thing to do.

SOPHIE: It won't hurt me. I just wanted to see.

MOTHER: What's there to see? It's dreadful outside.

SOPHIE: Yesterday there was still an aster in our garden. (*With a gesture of helplessness*) It's already—gone.

MOTHER: It's the end of October.—Come (*as she arranges the pillows*) lie down here so I can cover you.

SOPHIE: Lie down again.

MOTHER: You've been up on your feet for a while, taken a long walk to the window, and been as careless as ever. It's time for you to take a rest again.

SOPHIE (*obeys*): Take a rest.

MOTHER (*lays the warm, green blanket carefully over her*): How's that?

SOPHIE *nods.*

MOTHER: Would you like me to read the newspaper to you?

SOPHIE: No, thank you. It doesn't interest me. It's so far away from me, all that. I'd rather you told me . . .

MOTHER: Alright—what I started to say earlier. (*Brings up an armchair.*) You see, I'm putting a chair right next to you. And for now I'll sit down in it. But it's not for me. In half an hour, perhaps there'll be someone else sitting here—guess who?

SOPHIE: Why don't you just stay, Mama . . .

MOTHER: No, child, I have to go home. Besides, I've stayed out extra long today, and you'll like the person who's coming much better.

SOPHIE (*musing*): Better—no . . .

MOTHER: Oh, yes, I think so. Just guess.

*Pause.*

SOPHIE (*suddenly sitting up*): No—no. He mustn't come. He mustn't come. Tell him.

MOTHER *startled, looks at her questioningly.*

SOPHIE: I don't want to see him. It was a grave injustice. It was surely a sin.

MOTHER: Who are you talking about, child?

SOPHIE (*continuing her train of thought*): He buried her in consecrated ground and gave her last rites. And yet he knew she died in sin and by her own hand . . .

MOTHER: You mustn't condemn your old teacher.

SOPHIE: She died by her own hand.

MOTHER: He had compassion for her, and she was confused.

SOPHIE (*excited*): Why are all of you lying? You know the truth. Agla was as sane as you and I when she drowned herself . . . and the reverend was fully aware of it. No—I can't, I won't see him. Please!

MOTHER: Calm down, Sophie. He's not coming.—someone else . . .

SOPHIE (*breathing a sigh of relief*): Someone—else . . .

MOTHER (*listens*): And I think—he's here already.

SOPHIE (*listens, sits up, looks toward the door in suspense—it opens and Ernst rushes in quickly*): Ernst?

ERNST (*stops after a few steps*): Ah—how I've been running.

MOTHER (*to Sophie*): Now, isn't that a surprise.

SOPHIE (*not understanding*): Yes—why? . . .

ERNST (*greeting*): Well—good morning, Mama—good morning, Sophie. (*Kisses her hand and forehead.*) Today we had a little less work for once . . . and so I thought I'd . . . ? (*Stops, at a loss.*)

MOTHER: Well, now I can go with some peace of mind. I know I'm leaving you in good hands.

SOPHIE *embraces her mother fervently.*

MOTHER: There, my child. Now just lie there quietly. Be good. And you (*to Ernst*) be strict with her.

*She presents her hand to Ernst and catches his eye; they exchange a meaningful glance—Ernst starts to accompany her to the door.*

MOTHER: Stay where you are! Good-bye, children.

SOPHIE (*nods*): God bless you, Mama.

*Mother leaves.*

### Scene Three

### Sophie, Ernst

ERNST (*as he sits down*): May I?

SOPHIE: Wherever you like.

*Pause—the storm is heard.*

ERNST: The storm bothered me all last night.

SOPHIE: Yes, would you please have someone look upstairs. There must be a shutter loose somewhere. It's been banging so much against the house. It frightens me.

ERNST (*ready to get up*): Alright—I'll do it right away.

SOPHIE: Later—before you leave. It's only at night. (*Shivers.*)

ERNST (*sits back down*): As you wish.

SOPHIE *starts.*

ERNST: You're cold; shall I get you a shawl . . . ?

SOPHIE: Oh, no—it's nothing.

ERNST: By the way, we're really going to freeze out here—when winter comes. After all, we're practically out in the country— open to wind on all sides . . . And if you're not used to it . . .

*Pause.*

ERNST: If we can just get through the winter.

SOPHIE (*sighs*): Yes.

ERNST: It will be beautiful out here in the spring. When you have a little garden, you get closer to springtime. It's almost a feeling—of oneness with it.

SOPHIE *looks closely at him.*

ERNST: Are you looking forward to it, too?

SOPHIE (*wearily*): It's behind us already.

ERNST (*hesitating*): But before us as well, isn't it? . . .

*Pause.*

SOPHIE (*strokes his hair*): You poor thing.

ERNST: Poor?

SOPHIE (*impatiently*): You've been under such a strain these last few weeks. You must be tired.

ERNST: It will pass quickly.

SOPHIE (*rapidly*): Yes, and you shouldn't spend your little bit of free time sitting here. Here with me. In this dank, hospital air.

ERNST *disagrees.*

SOPHIE: I mean it. Why should you?—What if you were to get sick, too. Just think. Go for a walk, or to the cafe. You can meet some friends and have a good time. A healthy person belongs with healthy people. This is no relaxation for you— being here.

ERNST: Why do you hurt me this way, Sophie?

SOPHIE: I'm just telling the truth; it's no use. I'm not afraid; I'm not a child. I can stay here by myself.

ERNST: You won't have to do that anymore.

SOPHIE: Did mama say that? The dear! Just let her talk, but she doesn't understand anything about it. You go ahead!

ERNST (*warmly*): Please, Sophie. (*He seizes her hands.*)

SOPHIE: What?

ERNST: Let me stay.

*They look into each other's eyes for a moment. Then all of a sudden, Sophie violently pushes his hands away from her. In deep suffering.*

SOPHIE: You keep thinking about *her*. Right now you're thinking about her again. Why do you come begging to me?

ERNST (*perplexed*): Who am I thinking about, who? . . .

SOPHIE (*with increased anger and disgust*): Go. You can think about her in your office, all day. But spare me. Spare me. (*In desperation*) Don't you see that you violate me when you come into my room with these thoughts, that you humiliate me, that you make me suffer? (*She breaks into tears.*)

ERNST (*has stood up*): I don't understand you.

*Pause.*

SOPHIE (*raises her head; with sudden fury, she grabs her be-
wildered husband by the arm and pulls him to her, so that he is
sitting by her on the couch. Then she extends her hand*): Look,
can you see her? Here. She doesn't look so small in her green
dress, does she? Not at all like a child. And her black eyes,
how they shine. Do you see? Why is she smiling like this? You
must know why she's smiling like this, don't you? Does she
always smile this way? And she's let her hair down. She has
such beautiful, thick, black hair. And she's so pale, and yet her
lips are so red. As red as blood. She is coming to you. Softly.
And she is not at all like a child anymore—(*Her voice is
calmer; she takes a breath and asks in a tired voice*) Can you
see her?

ERNST (*at first looks in terror at Sophie; then he follows her hand
and her glance, and as she describes Agla, his eyes become
more and more attentive, and more and more filled with com-
prehension. He drinks in her words greedily; almost in ecstasy,
he continues to listen even after she has stopped; and in answer
to her last question, he says—believing*): Yes.

*Surprised and horrified, Sophie looks at his ecstatic face and
gestures a few times with her hands as if to ward him off, before
she collapses in deep suffering. Ernst continues to stare at the
phantom. The features grow darker and darker. Pause.*

ERNST (*in sudden realization*): Oh.—(*He runs his hand over his
forehead. Completely himself again*) Forgive me, I'm sorry.
(*He puts his arms around Sophie.*)

SOPHIE (*through her tears*): No, no. I'll let you go. You're in
love with her.

ERNST (*leaning over her*): No.

SOPHIE (*fading away*): You're in love with her.

ERNST: I'm just so afraid. Help me, Sophie. (*Shouting*) I'm
afraid!

SOPHIE (*straightens up and nestles close to him*): You're afraid?
I am, too.

*They cling to one another, terrified.*

ERNST (*trustingly*): Help me.

SOPHIE: You help me.

ERNST (*both of them confessing in a rush*): She's always there, isn't she?

SOPHIE (*nods*): Yes, always.

ERNST (*anxiously*): And at night?

SOPHIE (*weakly*): Yes.

ERNST: With you, too?

SOPHIE (*the same*): Yes.

ERNST: And yet she was so small?

SOPHIE: Yes.

ERNST: And delicate?

SOPHIE: Yes.

ERNST: And now?

SOPHIE: She's ghastly.

ERNST (*horrified*): Ghastly.

*Pause.*

SOPHIE: She bought you. You.

ERNST: Oh.

SOPHIE: She bought you.

ERNST: I don't want to. Help me.

SOPHIE (*full of regret*): You . . .

ERNST: Hold me tight. That's it. And now, tell me what we can do.

SOPHIE (*feebly*): I can't go on.

ERNST: Fight against her, together?

SOPHIE (*dejectedly*): No.

ERNST: Well—then—

SOPHIE (*they exchange a glance—liberated*): Yes.

ERNST: Together?

*Sophie nods. They cling to each other. Pause.*

SOPHIE (*rises in nameless horror—tonelessly*): Ernst!

ERNST *stands up.*

SOPHIE: We can't die.

ERNST *looks at her questioningly.*

SOPHIE (*with conviction*): Because *she* is there!

*Ernst drops heavily into the chair at the side of the couch, his hands over his face. Pause. Storm.*

*Scene Four*

*The same characters*

SOPHIE (*strokes his hair*): Darling.

ERNST *looks at her—his eyes become brighter and brighter.*

SOPHIE: Darling.

ERNST: Are you in pain?

SOPHIE *with a barely visible smile shakes her head.*

ERNST: *It* will save us . . .

SOPHIE (*softly, intensely*): Perhaps.

*Curtain*

# Everyday Life

*A Play in Two Acts*

*Characters:*

GEORGE MILLNER, *the painter*
SOPHIE, *his sister*
DR. LEUTHOLD
MASCHA, *the model*
HELEN
MRS. WEAVER

*Setting: A spacious studio. Beneath the very large window, a drawing board with unfinished copper plates and assorted tools. To the left, an easel. On it a canvas frame (turned around). In the center, another large easel, next to it a stool with various cups and pot-bellied bronze containers, containing paint brushes. A narrow cabinet with drawers for paints. On top of the cabinet, all sorts of odds and ends, such as a small mirror, a bottle of cognac, a few small glasses, a cigarette box, and a red Japanese bowl with tea cookies in it. Nearby a deep armchair with a very solid back and wide armrests, and turned toward it, as if in conversation, a red-varnished straw chair. The rear wall is taken up entirely by the window. On the wall to the left: a black cabinet, on it a skull wearing a cap, a small terra-cotta statue, containers, and a crown. On the wall itself, a number of sketches in charcoal, red ochre, and oil. Some framed, some not. In front, the stove, small, round, iron. On it some cooking utensils. Beside the cabinet,*

*the entryway from the landing. Wall to the right: near the window,
a couchette covered with a rug on which still other fabrics are
spread out, gold-embroidered and shining. The wall above it is
covered with green material up to a shelf which runs along about
halfway up. On the wall, several pictures. Above a small photo-
graph, fresh spring flowers. On the shelf a number of small, long-
stemmed Dutch pipes, arranged leaning in a row. Then small
sculptures, dolls, reliefs, and so forth. At the end of the couchette,
an ordinary door which leads into the bedroom. Next to it, in
front, a podium half hidden by a Spanish screen over which are
also thrown expensive coverings of crimson velvet, embroidered in
gold. Way up front, a very spacious table, used as a desk, covered
with papers, letters, books, and a number of odds and ends; next
to it a bookcase with light-colored books, mostly unbound. The
studio is located at the edge of town. It is early afternoon. Outside the window, gray, smooth rooftops, the clear spring sky, and
the gently moving top of a pinetree.*

# ACT ONE

GEORGE (*not very tall, about twenty-four years old, blond, with
soft hair and a small mustache, enters from the bedroom in a
black suit and black tie—smoothing and dusting off with his
hands the jacket which he obviously just has put on. Thus
absorbed he goes to the window. He looks out for awhile. Then
turns quickly, walks around the room as if he were looking
for something, finally finds the hand mirror on the narrow paint
cabinet, tries to see his tie in it, and makes an annoyed motion
because the mirror is quite dusty. Takes out his handkerchief,
wipes off the mirror, and throws the handkerchief on one of the
chairs. Then straightens his tie while he lifts up the mirror*):
There. (*Visibly relieved, takes a few steps toward the window.
He looks at his pocket watch.*) Ha . . . three o'clock . . . time—
lots of time. (*Steps back to the paint cabinet, which is only
about as high as a tall table, and takes the cigarette box.
Grumbles*) Dust! Whatever you touch! (*Takes out a cigarette.
A knock at the door; he says carelessly*) Yes (*and begins to*

*look for matches. He finds a box, takes one out, strikes it.
Knocking again. George calls out angrily)* Yes—come in!
*(Meanwhile the match goes out. He hurls it to the floor, takes
another, and looks without much interest toward the door as
he lights his cigarette. A girl in a straw hat and a simple black
dress enters slowly and hesitatingly. George, waving the match
in the air)* Thank you, no! Don't need a model. *(Turns away,
smokes.)*

MASCHA: Mr. Millner . . . I . . .

GEORGE *(turning around quickly)*: Mascha? Oh! Didn't even
recognize you. Wearing black? Well, what is it?

MASCHA: I just wanted to ask . . .

GEORGE: Oh. We haven't seen each other for quite awhile. You
doing alright?

MASCHA: Oh, I'm . . . I suppose so. But don't you need me at all
anymore?

GEORGE: I'm not working now. Won't you sit down for a moment?

MASCHA: Yes, but aren't you going out?

GEORGE: Why?

MASCHA *(pointing at the suit)*: Well, because you're so . . .

GEORGE: Oh yes, later; later I have to . . . well, sit down. Busy
these days?

MASCHA *(comes and sits in the straw chair. George kneels with
one leg on the arm of the other comfortable chair)*: Afraid
not, nobody's doing anything . . .

GEORGE *(smiling)*: Well, as you see, neither am I.

MASCHA *(also smiling)*: But what do you do all day?

GEORGE: I do what's expected, that is, I visit people, get invited
places . . .

MASCHA: Do you enjoy that all of a sudden?

GEORGE: No.

MASCHA: Then why . . .

GEORGE: Well, you see, what I would like to do, I *can't* do.

MASCHA: But your painting . . .?

GEORGE: That's just it—painting.

MASCHA: You can't . . .?

GEORGE: No.

MASCHA: Who would have thought! Last winter . . .

GEORGE: Last winter, well. On those dark November days . . . Well, you know . . . How often then I used to wait for daylight, when it was still twilight at eleven. I used to sit in such a fright. After all, a whole day could have slipped by without—day. And those hours I missed might have been just when it would have come to me. And now I sleep till noon, just so I won't have to face all that unused light which fills the window early every morning.

MASCHA: But isn't it also because you come home late?

*Pause.*

GEORGE (*seriously*): Also—because I come home late. Yes. One must seek—diversion . . .

MASCHA: Yes, diversion and then—direction . . .

GEORGE: What? What do you mean?

MASCHA (*embarrassed*): It came to me just because of the words . . .

GEORGE: Just because of the words . . . In the end you're rather smart, aren't you?

MASCHA (*laughs*): No, just the words . . . (*Hesitates uneasily.*)

GEORGE: Say, you've really learned a lot, haven't you?

MASCHA: Very little. Just when I started to read well, we became very poor.

GEORGE: All of a sudden?

MASCHA: Yes, overnight. Father played the stock market. And then . . .

GEORGE: I see. Well, but you could read then, couldn't you?

MASCHA: Yes, I knew how to read from then on. Before, I'd always stood in front of father's books and thought to myself: if only I could read. And when I finally could . . .

GEORGE: Well, when you finally could, what then?

MASCHA: We didn't have any more books.

GEORGE: Oh, they took everything away from you.

MASCHA: Yes, they took everything away from us.

GEORGE: And then?

MASCHA: Well, then . . . (*Sadly*)

GEORGE: If you ever want to borrow some of those books over there . . . (*Points at the bookcase.*)

MASCHA: Oh, I'd like that! I often meant to ask you.

*Pause.*

GEORGE: There isn't much there, actually. But maybe you'll find something anyway. (*Pause*) Why are you looking at me like that?

MASCHA: You look just the way you used to.

GEORGE: When?

MASCHA: In November, when you were painting.

GEORGE: When I was painting . . .

MASCHA: Yes, so . . . so . . . humble . . .

GEORGE: What?

MASCHA: It's not the right expression. No. I don't mean that at all.

GEORGE: What then?

MASCHA: You have a working face and—and—another one.

GEORGE (*puts his cigarette in the ash tray*): Hm! And the working face, what is it like?

MASCHA (*calmly*): Devout.

GEORGE *looks at her soberly.*

MASCHA *gets up.*

GEORGE: And today I have that—that face?

MASCHA: Yes.

*Pause.*

GEORGE (*smiling*): Then I suppose I'll be needing you again very soon.

MASCHA (*overjoyed*): Oh yes!

GEORGE (*hesitatingly*): Maybe. (*He begins to pace nervously back and forth.*) Maybe. I do have plans, all the time . . . but they get in each other's way . . . But occasionally . . . Last week, for example, on a rainy day: toward evening it suddenly turned golden, fairytale golden—after a rainy day. The ground warm and heavy . . . in the distance. And up close, everything shimmering, in clear contours, so simple, so touchingly simple . . . That was last week on Thursday, and then: well, if only one had the courage to begin right away, to begin right away, every time. But then one thinks about it . . .

MASCHA: And seeks diversion.

GEORGE (*stops, looks at her*): You're right, I'll call you soon, Mascha.

MASCHA: Tomorrow!

GEORGE: Tomorrow?—That soon? Hardly. I'll be coming home late . . . and this place will have to be dusted . . . and . . . You see how it all looks.

MASCHA *quickly takes off her hat and coat.*

GEORGE: What now?

MASCHA: Dusting. Do you have any rags?

GEORGE: What, you want to do that now?

MASCHA: Yes, right away. Where are the rags?

GEORGE: But . . .

MASCHA *in the meantime has opened up the cabinet on the left and started looking.*

GEORGE (*pulling open the bottom drawer of the paint cabinet*): Here, here.

*He throws her two dust rags, and she begins immediately to wipe off the cabinet and to put things in order so that they are not pedantically but tastefully arranged. George lights up another cigarette and then leans against the drawing board. His back to the window. He watches her.*

MASCHA (*kneeling by one of the easels, keeping busy, softly*): But maybe you'll need one *with a face* this time?

GEORGE: What do you mean? (*Smokes.*)

MASCHA (*dusts, standing the pictures against the wall to the left*): In my case, only the arms and legs are worth anything . . .

GEORGE *studies her.*

MASCHA *turns back to him questioning, since he is silent.*

GEORGE (*in sudden haste, throwing away his cigarette and rushing to the easel*): Stop, for God's sake, stay, stay like that . . . (*The model calmly maintains her pose while George rushes around the studio tossing frames and drawing-boards around, puts a frame on the easel, tears open the cabinet, takes out a box of charcoal, and begins to work with lightning strokes in front of the easel. Caught up in his work*): There, there . . . you can let your arms down now . . . (*He unbuttons his coat and throws it on the floor.*)

MASCHA *does not move.*

GEORGE (*keeps on working*): Just let your arms go. I only need your face . . .

MASCHA *slowly, as if paralyzed by astonishment, lowers her arms.*

GEORGE *works.*

MASCHA *suddenly, with a violent gesture, covers her face with her hands.*

GEORGE: But Mascha! Mascha! Damn it, you're ruining it for me! . . .

MASCHA *sobs.*

GEORGE (*throws the charcoal away*): Well, so much for that . . .

MASCHA (*shaken*): No, no—I'm sorry—I—(*She removes her hands and tries to duplicate the former pose of her head.*)

GEORGE (*angry*): Yes, of course, that's it . . . Why the devil can't you keep still?

MASCHA (*quite embarrassed*): I'm sorry . . . I . . .

GEORGE: You're sorry! So much for that . . . your face is all wet . . . That does it.

MASCHA *remains standing sadly.*

GEORGE: That does it, I tell you! (*He throws the frame against the wall. Then he notices he is in shirtsleeves, picks up his coat and puts it on again.*)

MASCHA *approaches him.*

GEORGE: What now?

MASCHA (*embarrassed*): Your coat, Mr. . . . it's all dusty now . . .

GEORGE: Well, then brush me off.

MASCHA *looks for the brush.*

GEORGE (*points toward the table*): There.

MASCHA *takes it and brushes him off. Pause, at that moment a knock at the door.*

GEORGE (*loudly*): Come in!

SOPHIE (*through the crack in the door*): May I?

GEORGE: That you, Sophie?

SOPHIE: Yes, it's me.

GEORGE: Come on in, sis.

MASCHA *stops brushing, looks toward the door, afraid.*

SOPHIE *an older girl, simply dressed, her hair parted, not pretty but tender, with intelligent and kind eyes that show understanding. She shuts the door behind her and hesitates when she sees Mascha.*

GEORGE: Evening! Come on in. This is Mascha. You remember. She's just brushing my coat off. I have to go to Mallings for dinner.

SOPHIE (*comes forward*): Good evening, George. (*To Mascha*) Good evening.

*She offers her hand. Mascha notices this, quickly and softly puts her hand in Sophie's, but just for a second. She is visibly astonished by Sophie's friendliness. Then she immediately finds something to do, puts the dust rags into the still-open drawer of the paint cabinet, and rushes off to get her hat and coat.*

SOPHIE: Where did you say you were going?

GEORGE (*offers her a seat on the couchette, pulls the straw chair up for himself*): To Mallings.

SOPHIE (*sits down on the couchette*): Oh, yes, isn't young Malling getting married today?

GEORGE (*sits down with his back partly to the audience*): Yes, that's it. I'm not going to the wedding because I don't like these ceremonies. But I couldn't quite get out of the dinner afterwards. Young Malling has taken a liking toward me lately and would be offended. Especially since only a very small circle has been invited. Formal attire isn't even required, as you can see. But what about you, what have you been doing? Are you all right, and mama?

SOPHIE (*smiling*): Ah, mama sent me here. She hasn't seen you for three days, so she's worried. You know how she is. Besides, she had a dream about you last night, and now she imagines that something must have happened to you. Old people become superstitious when they're not feeling well—you know.—You're alright?

GEORGE: Yes—unless you want to add chronic laziness to your list of ailments.

SOPHIE (*smiling*): Well, at least not among the fatal ones . . .

GEORGE (*seriously*): Oh, but it is! In a way . . . (*Pause*) But you can tell mama that I'm going to Mallings, that is, actually to the Hotel Europe; that's where the banquet is taking place. And what else is mama doing?

SOPHIE: Oh—same as ever. But I think the young lady—Mascha wants something . . . (*She motions her head toward Mascha,*

*who is standing in the doorway with her hat and coat on, hesi-
tating and undecided.*)

MASCHA: I just wanted to say . . . I'm going now.

GEORGE (*gets up slightly, halfway turning toward her*): Alright,
alright. Bye, Mascha.

SOPHIE: Bye.

MASCHA: Good evening, Miss Millner. (*Leaves.*)

SOPHIE: So that's Mascha? The famous Mascha.

GEORGE (*absentmindedly*): Yes, Mascha.

SOPHIE: The one you told me about in November, when you were
painting your great picture . . .

GEORGE (*suddenly gets up, hastily*): Excuse me, one moment.

SOPHIE: Of course . . .

GEORGE (*hurries to the door, opens it, and calls out*): Mascha!

*Pause. On the staircase, footsteps cease.*

GEORGE: Mascha!

MASCHA (*from below*): Yes, coming.

*Hastily approaching footsteps are heard; Mascha obviously has
returned but remains unseen outside the door; George speaks
through the doorway.*

GEORGE: I just wanted to tell you, Mascha: It's alright. What
happened, you know.

MASCHA (*out of breath from running*): Oh—I was so ashamed
. . .

GEORGE: Ashamed? Well, anyway, as I said: No harm done.
Maybe it isn't ruined after all. I do have the sketch, and I still
have it in my head, too. Why don't you come back tomorrow.

MASCHA (*with incredulous joy*): Really?

GEORGE (*calmly*): Yes, early, at eight or eight-thirty. Is that
alright?

MASCHA: Yes, oh yes.

GEORGE: Fine then.—Bye. (*Shuts the door and returns quickly.*)
I'm sorry . . . a small matter between us had to be cleared up.

SOPHIE: You really are industrious, then . . . You actually want
to begin at eight?

GEORGE: No, no, I was just trying to . . . You see, Mascha
thought . . . By the way, it was nice of you to offer her your
hand . . .

SOPHIE: Oh!—She was practically an old acquaintance to me, from all your stories. You talked about her a lot last winter. And she's not actually a model, like the others, I mean.

GEORGE: No, no . . .

SOPHIE: She's not even *pretty*, is she?

GEORGE: Did I ever say she was?

SOPHIE (*smiling*): No. But that's the way I always pictured her. With a serious, calm face, a bit pale; beautiful, silent lips, proud forehead and eyes . . . Her eyes, anyway, are almost the way I imagined them.

GEORGE (*quickly*): Yes, aren't they, those eyes! I noticed them today, too! (*Pause*) But perhaps you weren't wrong about the rest, either . . .

SOPHIE *looks at him questioningly.*

GEORGE: What I mean is: maybe that's what the face of her soul looks like. (*Pause. Suddenly*) Say, Leuthold could come at any moment. It won't be unpleasant for you to meet him, will it?

SOPHIE: Unpleasant? No.

GEORGE: Well, I just meant, after you turn someone down . . .

SOPHIE: Oh, we can be friends; of course, he can't visit us anymore now. Mama would find that strange. But after all, there aren't any rules of behavior set down for how two people who *didn't* get married are supposed to act. And for precisely that reason, it should be possible to build a relationship with no prescribed regulations, free from all conventions. Don't you think so?

GEORGE: Bravo! That's a great idea! That's even my idea. My life's work, so to speak.

SOPHIE: Isn't that a rather limited goal for an entire lifetime?

GEORGE: How do you mean?

SOPHIE: Well, aren't all real relationships like that, free from all conventions.

GEORGE: Oh, what blissful ignorance!

SOPHIE: No, I'm not joking, ours, for instance.

GEORGE: Ours, hm? Would you come up here to the studio if you weren't my sister?

SOPHIE: Well, what would I be then?

GEORGE: Oh, a lady, and acquaintance, a friend . . .

SOPHIE: A friend?

GEORGE: Aha, you see . . .

SOPHIE (*laughing*): Alright, I would come, to *you* I would come.

GEORGE (*laughing*): Alright, alright . . . I believe you. (*Pause. Solemnly*) If only you would come!

SOPHIE (*not understanding*): George?

GEORGE: I'm lonely, very, very lonely. I've even thought about whether I should move in with you and mama. You still have a guest room. Maybe I'm just so lonesome here, being in this large, empty room. Then we could really be together. Mama and you and I. How about in the evening. We could read; well, in that light it would be a strain on the eyes. We could talk then—tell stories—perhaps even sit quietly . . . That's quite different from being quiet and alone . . . I often imagine that we're sitting together like that . . . (*He hesitates, noticing Sophie's doubting look.*) Hm?

SOPHIE: George, I'm afraid you don't mean *us* . . .

GEORGE (*astonished*): Not you? Who then?

SOPHIE: Well . . . the result of your life's work . . .

GEORGE (*with a negating gesture of his hand, then after a pause, warmly*): I'd like to help you, Sophie.

SOPHIE (*looking quite astonished*): Help me?!

GEORGE: Oh, I know it's not easy for you, being with mother all day, year after year . . . Her age makes her ungrateful, her suffering makes her moody. I can imagine what that means . . .

SOPHIE: Shall I tell you something, George . . . I see it now: quite unintentionally, I had the same goal in life as you.

GEORGE *looks at her questioningly.*

SOPHIE: To build a relationship free from all conventions. (*More softly*) I left my mother a long time ago, George, but I found a human being, a poor unhappy human being, whom I serve, and to whom I am everything. For in the evening I close the curtains in her room and make it night, and then shortly before noon, I open the shutters and make it day again. And my hands bring her food and medicine, and my voice, softly reading, brings her sleep . . . You reminded me that this human being is my mother . . .

GEORGE (*offers his hand, warmly*): *Our* mother!

SOPHIE (*takes his hand. They look into each other's eyes. Pause*):
Mother's expecting me.

GEORGE: But now you won't see Leuthold after all.

SOPHIE: It's a shame—but it's getting late. Does he visit you
often?

GEORGE: No, he's not very sociable, as you know; but today he
promised to fetch me for the dinner party . . .

SOPHIE: Is he a friend of the Mallings, too?

GEORGE: Yes, though I think more so of Baron Malling than
Rolf. He belongs, so to speak, to another generation.

SOPHIE: Yes, yes, that happens so quickly now . . .

GEORGE: Yes . . . although the young . . . (*A knock*) Ah, that
could be him. Come in—So it is!

DR. LEUTHOLD (*enters. A slender man*):   Good evening! (*He is
startled when he notices Sophie, does not immediately recognize her because of his nearsightedness, and says suddenly*)
Oh, Miss Millner.

SOPHIE (*approaches him and offers her hand*): Hello, Dr.
Leuthold. We were just discussing whether you belong to the
old or new generation.

DR. LEUTHOLD (*shakes hands with George, then as he removes his
pince nez*): To neither, if you please. But if I must be classi-
fied, place me with the old. I should like to hold back to see if
there really will be a new one.

SOPHIE: What, you think . . .?

DR. LEUTHOLD: I don't think the old ruins have become something
new already.

GEORGE: But you admit, at least, that the old is on its way out?

SOPHIE: And that in this process no injustice is being done to
the old?

DR. LEUTHOLD: You ask too much of me. Possibly it's quite
superfluous to tear things down, since the new may not be able
to grow in this exhausted ground, so burdened by ruins—but
somewhere else instead, in new and youthful soil . . .

SOPHIE: You think, then, there is that much room in the world?

DR. LEUTHOLD: Oh—and if someday there is no more land still
untouched, then it will rise up from the sea, the new . . .

GEORGE: You are a poet, Doctor.

DR. LEUTHOLD: But an old-fashioned one, whom you surely would not read.

GEORGE: Oh, I—I don't read any poets at all. I mean, on the whole—I like a few lines by some, and although they are all different poets—romantics and decadents, French, Italian, German, Russian—all my favorite poems often seem to me to be by *one* poet—so similar are they.

DR. LEUTHOLD: After all, there is *one* poet behind them all.

GEORGE: Oh . . . you mean—God?

DR. LEUTHOLD: Do *you?*

GEORGE (*confused*): I don't know. (*Pause*)

DR. LEUTHOLD (*looks at his watch*): But I think . . .

GEORGE (*as if waking up*): Yes, of course—it's time. Is your carriage outside?

DR. LEUTHOLD: Yes.

GEORGE: Won't you sit down for just a moment! Sophie, offer the doctor some cigarettes. You know where they are. I'll be with you right away. (*Hurries into the bedroom.*)

SOPHIE (*points toward the armchair*): Please sit down. Do you smoke?

DR. LEUTHOLD: No, thank you. Not now. Not before dinner . . .

SOPHIE *fetches the straw chair for herself.*

DR. LEUTHOLD (*hastening to her*): Oh, I'm sorry, Miss Millner. (*Wants to help her.*)

SOPHIE: Thank you, Dr. Leuthold. I'm used to helping myself. (*She sits down.*)

DR. LEUTHOLD *sits down in the armchair, erect, without leaning back. Pause.*

SOPHIE: Are you a friend of the Mallings?

DR. LEUTHOLD: Well acquainted. I have dealt with the old baron frequently in my capacity as a physician . . . And furthermore, I know the family of young Malling's bride.

SOPHIE: Then you have connections with both families. And you didn't go to the ceremony?

DR. LEUTHOLD: No, I don't like to watch people getting married.

SOPHIE: Are you afraid of that dreadful sight?

DR. LEUTHOLD: I find this sort of public display unpleasant.

SOPHIE: In your opinion one should marry quietly?

DR. LEUTHOLD: Yes, as inconspicuously as possible. As far as I'm concerned, one can let oneself be buried with lots of ceremony; for no one envies the dead.

SOPHIE: That's true, no one envies the dead. How nice to hear you say that.

DR. LEUTHOLD: Why?

SOPHIE: Because it means you enjoy being alive.

DR. LEUTHOLD (*smiling*): I'm alive.

SOPHIE: Well, that's enough. You don't belong to the old generation, Dr. Leuthold.

DR. LEUTHOLD: There's no life left in it? (*Smiling*)

SOPHIE (*hesitating*): Not like that . . .

GEORGE (*enters wearing an overcoat, with hat and gloves in hand*): Well—here I am. Shall we go?

DR. LEUTHOLD *gets up.*

SOPHIE: Yes, it's high time, isn't it, George?

GEORGE: Well, we'll be there in a couple of minutes.

SOPHIE (*to Dr. Leuthold*): Good-bye then, Dr. Leuthold. It's too bad that you have to leave so soon. Perhaps chance will bring us together here again sometime.

DR. LEUTHOLD: And you would have no suspicions concerning such an act of chance?

SOPHIE: No, because ultimately every chance is governed by law.

DR. LEUTHOLD: And you respect laws?

SOPHIE: Yes, certain laws, for instance . . .

GEORGE: For instance?

SOPHIE: For instance, the laws of friendship.

*She offers him her hand.*

DR. LEUTHOLD (*respectfully kisses the hand that is offered him*): Thank you very, very much.

SOPHIE: Until next time.

DR. LEUTHOLD: Yes, until next time.

GEORGE: But at least we're all going down the stairs together. After you, please. (*He opens the door and lets Sophie and Dr. Leuthold go first, then he follows.*)

*The stage remains empty for a few minutes. Then the door is unlocked from outside and in comes Mascha, the model, and a woman with broom, bucket, and washrags.*

MASCHA (*cheerfully*): There, Mrs. Weaver. I knew that the custodian would have the key. Just come on it. We have to hurry. It will be light for another two hours, and in that time the main work must be done. You can start right here . . . by the stove.

MRS. WEAVER (*imperiously*): Yes, it's already late. And the size of this room . . . It would make more sense tomorrow . . .

MASCHA (*impatiently*): No, no, that won't do—by tomorrow everything must be spic and span.

MRS. WEAVER (*putting on her apron*): I see! (*She carries the cleaning equipment into the room.*) You're going to have something special here tomorrow, hm? . . .

MASCHA (*already intent on cleaning off the table, with a beaming smile*): Yes, Mrs. Weaver, something special.

*Curtain*

## ACT TWO

*The morning of the following day. George is sitting in the comfortable armchair smoking, drinking coffee, and leafing through a portfolio of sketches. A knock at the door.*

GEORGE: Yes?

MASCHA: Good morning.

GEORGE: Ah, Mascha. Come right in.

MASCHA *quickly comes forward.*

GEORGE (*calmly continues to leaf through the sketches*): I'm afraid we won't be working today . . .

MASCHA (*startled*): No?

GEORGE: No. (*Smiling*) Or does it look to you as though I'm wearing my working face?

MASCHA: It's not that—but . . .

GEORGE: But what?

MASCHA: You look so happy.

GEORGE: I am. Something happened to me, something that . . .

MASCHA: Yesterday?

GEORGE: Yes, very late. A surprise.

MASCHA: And that's why you're so happy. Really?

GEORGE: Yes—

MASCHA: But it was such a little thing . . .

GEORGE *looks up quizzically.*

MASCHA (*embarrassed*): Not anything worth mentioning. I just thought that if we were going to be working here today . . .

GEORGE: You mean? . . .

MASCHA: Well, that's why I straightened up everything here . . . but really, Mr. Millner, it's nothing worth mentioning.

GEORGE (*looks around in amazement, noticing for the first time that the studio is in sparkling order*): Ah, yes, of course.

MASCHA: But you didn't even notice . . .

GEORGE (*quickly, when he sees her dismayed expression*): Of course I did, of course. I just meant *that, too.* Really, a surprise. Very nice.—Thanks, Mascha.

MASCHA (*looking away, distantly*): You're welcome.

GEORGE: It's really appropriate, particularly today. I want everything to look special today.

MASCHA: Then you want to work after all? (*Turns toward him.*)

GEORGE: No, not work. I'm expecting a visitor.

MASCHA: Oh?

GEORGE: Yes, a lady.

MASCHA: Oh?

GEORGE: Yes, a young lady.

MASCHA: You want to paint her?

GEORGE: That too, that too . . . Possibly I'll paint her, also. (*Musing*) Well, it was really strange yesterday. I'll tell you about it . . . You've got time, haven't you?

MASCHA: I've got plenty of time.

GEORGE: Well, sit down then.

MASCHA *remains standing.*

GEORGE: I'm sure you can imagine what goes on at dinners like that. They're stiff and boring. And especially a wedding dinner. Tasteless toasts, constant embarrassment, and silly laughter. Naturally I didn't expect anything else. But once I got there, once I got in the mood, you know, I talked a great deal, then this strange thing happened.

MASCHA: The surprise.

GEORGE: Yes, the surprise. She understood me. I mean she really understood me, beyond the mere words . . . do you understand? We were seeing each other for the first time and immediately, without all the introductions, without all the conventions. One human being to another. You can't imagine what that means. After dinner we withdrew into a corner and told each other about ourselves. It was almost like reliving certain details, because we basically knew everything about each other. Everything that mattered. Isn't that odd?

MASCHA (*tries to smile*): Oh yes, it must really have . . .

GEORGE: What?

MASCHA: I mean, that sort of thing must be very rare.

GEORGE: Think of all the things that usually have to happen before you get to know a person. Violent emotions, misunderstandings, sometimes even deaths are necessary. Usually you have to break into people, attack them at a time when they won't defend themselves. You have to do it quickly and violently, with a pretext for them to keep their doors open. But here: Everything was open, and lo and behold—there I was. And . . . (*He looks up.*) Did you want to say something?

MASCHA: Oh no, I was just thinking . . . something like that must be very beautiful.

GEORGE: Very beautiful, Mascha, very beautiful. Think of coming into a person when everything is calm inside. Not having to enter by storm and in uncertainty, the way it usually is. To come into tranquility, a quiet room, as if everything had been prepared for you.

MASCHA: Yes, yes.

GEORGE: You understand me?

MASCHA (*tries to smile*): A little.

GEORGE (*smiles, distracted*): Good, good! I'm saying so many things, which actually . . . But for once I feel the need to find the right words for everything and to hear these words. I suppose I would be saying all this even if I were alone . . .

MASCHA: Oh—(*sadly*) then it doesn't bother you that I'm here.

GEORGE: No, no . . .(*Preoccupied*) And do you know what an advantage it is to get to know someone this way, when they have peace of mind?—You see them the way they really are . . .

MASCHA: The way they really are?

GEORGE: Yes, you can't make a mistake then.

MASCHA (*confused*): Oh, of course . . . (*Quickly*) Then you think a mistake is out of the question—under these circumstances?

GEORGE: Yes, out of the question. We would find it just as natural to live together as yesterday it was natural to tell each other about ourselves.

MASCHA (*suppresses her apprehension, then quickly*): And she, I mean the lady, so she told you about herself, too?

GEORGE: Yes, later, toward the end. I spoke first, and then afterwards, when I had told everything, she began—quite intimately, as if to an old friend. About her childhood, her parents. Incidentally, they're both dead. She's all alone. And perhaps it was only possible because of that . . .

MASCHA: What?

GEORGE: This curious confidence in another person.

MASCHA: Because she's so alone, this lady?

GEORGE: Yes, alone—like me . . .

MASCHA: . . . like . . .?

GEORGE: Like me—or (*smiling*) like you. Actually, you're all alone, too.

MASCHA (*forces a laugh*): Oh me, why I . . . I have lots of friends! . . .

GEORGE (*scarcely notices her laugh*): Yesterday, who would have guessed. (*He stands up.*)

MASCHA (*sad again*): Yes, yesterday no one would have imagined such a thing.

GEORGE: That's life. And that's the beauty of it. The unexpected. (*Pause*)

MASCHA: Yes, my father has often said: there's something beautiful in an unexpected death.

GEORGE (*looks at her*): What made you say that?

MASCHA: Oh, just something I remembered.

GEORGE: Don't you have any happy memories?

MASCHA (*tries to say something. Then quickly*): Well . . . now I have to . . .

GEORGE: So soon?—Well, I'll be seeing you.

MASCHA (*backs away a few steps*): Not for awhile now, I suppose, Mr. Millner.

GEORGE: Why?

MASCHA: Well, now nothing will become of our . . . our work, I mean . . .

GEORGE (*has gone to the window, without turning around*): Yes —you may be right . . . (*Suddenly lively, comes forward a few steps.*) On the other hand, last night, during my conversation with Helen, everything seemed to fall into place. I told her—all about the paintings, you know.

MASCHA: Including . . . including the one from last November?

GEORGE: Yes, but especially about the ones to come. After all, she practically knows the old ones, at least in her mind . . .

MASCHA *looks at him questioningly.*

GEORGE: Well—I mean, just like the rest of my past, through my rapidly told stories that became so strangely familiar to her. But mostly we talked about the pictures I have yet to paint, the future: *That's* what we really had to talk about.

MASCHA (*softly*): Oh—all at once? . . .

GEORGE: Yes . . . You see . . . there was a picture. Emigrants: a level field behind the harvest crop, poor, meager. And people going away, into the setting sun, a crowd huddled together, dark. Many backs, bent as if under the burden of their own silhouettes . . . And then she said: "As if they were turning into mountains at the edge of the world . . ." And that was exactly right. That's just what my picture meant: they were turning into mountains at the edge of the world. (*Pause*) And then there was something else: I called it "Christ." And she understood immediately that I didn't mean a figure, a person, but a landscape. The hereafter heralded by anticipation . . . Oh, Mascha, I just wish I could begin! (*With a grand gesture*)

MASCHA: Yes, that must be the hardest part.

GEORGE: An immense effort, that's what it is! Nothing has happened, a morning just like any other. And then you step to your desk, or your easel, and—it comes, the inconceivable. You express what only can be actually imagined as silence. Yet you express it, you shout it out loud, hot and breathlessly, as if before you there stood thousands who would starve to death without this word . . .

MASCHA (*softly, almost inaudible*): There are *more* than thousands . . .

GEORGE: You can't understand all that, child. (*Tired, his hand over his eyes.*)

MASCHA (*calmly*): No.

GEORGE: Are you leaving already? (*He walks over to the paint cabinet, lights a cigarette.*) Well, good-bye for now, Helen will be here any minute anyway. I'll write to you if I should need you.

MASCHA: If you should need me, right?

GEORGE: Yes, a postcard. (*Offers his hand.*)

MASCHA *takes it.*

GEORGE: Are you cold? (*As if he noticed her for the first time*) You don't look well today. Didn't you get any sleep?

MASCHA: Not much.

GEORGE (*lets go her hand. Superficially*): Still carnival time?

MASCHA (*sadly*): Always, all year long . . .

GEORGE (*laughs*): I see . . . Well, just don't get too much of a good thing! Goodbye.

MASCHA: Goodbye, Mr. Millner. (*Leaves quickly.*)

GEORGE (*remains standing and smoking at the writing table, looks around the room. As soon as Mascha has opened the door, quickly*): And thank you again for putting things in order here . . . But you know, you could . . . when will you be coming by here again?

MASCHA: Come by here? . . . I have to meet mother at noon . . . but in two hours . . .

GEORGE: In two hours, fine. You know, then you could bring some flowers for Helen with you. Would you mind?

MASCHA (*hesitating*): For? . . .

GEORGE: Yes, for the lady. I don't have any in the house, and they would look nice. I can't go out myself, Helen may come at any minute. And I don't want to send the woman downstairs, she always brings daisies. Every time I send her, she brings daisies, it's an obsession with her . . . Look for something pretty. Alright?

MASCHA (*softly*): Roses?

GEORGE: Whatever you like. You have good taste. The lady is blonde, about like you, you can judge from that.

MASCHA: Flowers for her hair? . . .

GEORGE (*impatiently*): God—maybe for her hair. I don't know. (*Pause. Mascha is about to leave.*) And listen, bring some fruit, too. Summer's just around the corner. Get some oranges, really ripe, dark ones. With a sweet southern summer hidden in them, all folded up inside . . . Would you? . . . In about two hours then? . . .

MASCHA: Yes, flowers and oranges. (*Opens the door.*)

GEORGE: And come right on in. So you can see her.

MASCHA: I'm to see her? (*With a trace of hostility*)

GEORGE: Why not?

MASCHA: It's just . . . I . . . flowers and oranges, then.

GEORGE: Yes, yes. Good-bye.

MASCHA *exits.*

GEORGE (*slowly paces up and down the room. Stops in front of several pictures, looks at them without paying attention, paces some more, then rushes suddenly to his desk, turns everything upside-down, finally finds a brush in a bag on the wall, brushes his coat. A knock at the door. Keeps on brushing vigorously and throws the brush aside, takes two or three giant steps toward the door and calls out*): Come in!

HELEN *in very elegant street attire, blonde, very sophisticated, no longer very young.*

GEORGE *stares at her briefly.*

HELEN: Well, don't you recognize me?

GEORGE (*beside himself*): Helen, I've been waiting for you, but . . .

HELEN (*peels off her right glove before offering him her exquisite but ringless hand*): I recognized you immediately.

GEORGE (*places his hand in hers. Still perplexed*): Recognized?

HELEN: Well, yes, in a way. We've never seen each other by daylight, after all.

GEORGE (*relieved*): Yes, that's true. And besides, imagine, I really expected you to wear a veil.

HELEN: Oh, you mean for a visit like this? . . .

GEORGE: Oh, but . . . how can you think such a thing? No, for some reason or other, I just imagined . . .

HELEN: I can hardly believe anyone saw me come in, so you don't have to worry.

GEORGE (*confused*): No, I . . . Please, won't you—(*He motions her into the room.*)

HELEN (*laughing*): You almost called me Miss Helen just now, didn't you? (*Comes forward.*)

GEORGE: I, no, really . . .

HELEN: Or perhaps even by my last name? (*She sits down in the comfortable chair.*)

GEORGE (*seriously*): Yes, to tell the truth, I did almost call you by your last name just now.

HELEN (*drolly*): So this is what it's come to! (*They laugh.*)

GEORGE: You smoke, don't you? (*He hands her the cigarette box.*)

HELEN (*as she takes out a cigarette*): Today you may still call me Helen.

GEORGE (*looks at her in amazement*): Today? . . . And then?

HELEN: Then what?—Give me a light. Please.

GEORGE: Yes—but tell me—(*Immobile*)

HELEN: Well, then I'll have to light the cigarette myself.

GEORGE (*quickly lights a match*): Excuse me, but . . . (*Suddenly, as if in a flash of insight*) Perhaps your name is not really Helen.

HELEN (*puffs her cigarette*): Quite to the contrary, that's my name . . .

GEORGE: I am curious . . .

HELEN: Don't make me smoke by myself. Why don't you sit down—

GEORGE (*does so quickly*): Alright, I'm sitting now . . .

HELEN (*smiling*): Comfortable?

GEORGE (*laughing*): Oh, yes . . .

HELEN (*looks around slowly*): Nice.

GEORGE: I beg your pardon?

HELEN: It's nice here. It's easy to imagine you working here. (*She puts her cigarette aside and extends her hands to him. With warmth*) I have been looking forward so much to getting to know this room. Everything here.

GEORGE (*jumping up*): Really?

HELEN (*calmly*): Yes, it was still necessary to see the stage.

GEORGE: Which stage?

HELEN: The one on which our lives slipped away . . .

GEORGE: Our . . .?

HELEN: Our lives of yesterday . . .

GEORGE: I'm sorry, but you say all that so strangely.

HELEN (*lets go of his hands and leans back*): Perhaps I'm expressing myself a bit clumsily. But that's excusable. Words are not meant for such things.

GEORGE: What do you mean?

HELEN: What did you think we would do today, George?

GEORGE: Do? Don't you know?

HELEN: Yes, *I* know . . . the question is what you think.

GEORGE: Well . . . I . . . I thought that today we would begin . . .

HELEN: Begin what?

GEORGE: Well, *It*—the things that matter, doing things together . . .

HELEN: Begin—again?

GEORGE: Yes, you're right. We did that yesterday—well, then, continue, expand, in a word, live!

HELEN: Live—all over again?

GEORGE (*steps back*): What—?

HELEN: Didn't you perceive that yesterday we had everything?

GEORGE *stares at her.*

HELEN (*extends her hands in defense, as if to ward off the astonishment in his eyes*): Yes, now that horror is coming over you, the same one that seized me yesterday. That nameless fear . . .

GEORGE (*in a monotone and with difficulty*): Fear?

HELEN: When you did not stop. When you took me along with you into this fleeting life, where past, present, and future no longer could be distinguished, like individual logs in one great flame. When you used up all our togetherness, even what was yet to come . . . I wanted to stop you. Enough! Not now, not here! Not all at once. Let us live it instead . . . later . . . Oh— but you didn't listen to me. You carried me along with you. You, you wanted to have everything—everything . . . (*Slowly, sadly*) And so I gave you everything.

GEORGE (*stares at her for a moment, then rushes to her, kneels, and grabs her by the shoulders*): Helen! (*Shouting*)

HELEN (*takes his head in her hands, tries to look into his eyes ... and gazes seriously into them for a moment, then softly, very sadly*): Even *that!* (*Pause*)

GEORGE (*in sudden bliss, wildly embracing her*): But darling, darling! What are you talking about? We were with people, in a crowd, not alone for a second. Don't you remember?

HELEN (*gently*): In spite of that, George, it's still as if it happened ... You forced me to open myself up to you ...

GEORGE *slowly lets her go.*

HELEN: I know all your gestures. Your tenderness and your force. Nothing can surprise me now. And you knew, too, for a moment, when our hands brushed, that I was naked and in your arms.

GEORGE (*helpless*): Forgive ...

HELEN (*leans forward to him*): That's not the way I mean it, George. It was happiness. It was real. And it was beautiful.

GEORGE (*trembling, raises his eyes. Then beseechingly*): Helen! (*Suddenly he lays his head in her lap.*)

HELEN (*strokes his hair*): Only, you see—I can't have your baby, George. But everything else *has* happened. Really. There is only *one* reality.

GEORGE *sobs.*

HELEN: Don't, George, don't. You wanted it to happen.

GEORGE (*softly*): No, not this way ...

HELEN: How then?

GEORGE: In real life ... here ...

HELEN: But then it might have turned into something imperfect.

GEORGE: And this way? ...

HELEN: Don't you feel it, too: we have lived together on an island for a long time, for a long time.

GEORGE (*raises his head*): Yes.

HELEN: And loved and kissed each other.

GEORGE: And won't do it any more?

HELEN (*smiling*): No ...

GEORGE: And why not?

HELEN: Because we no longer are on that island ... once again we are where everything has substance and shadow. And where the years pass between the individual events, like wide paths. And this is why we have to part.

GEORGE (*desperately*): Part?

HELEN: Yes, *there* parting did not exist. That belongs to *this* time. It is the only thing that remains for us. (*Pause*)

GEORGE (*gets up*): Helen, you can't believe all this was just an overture in which each leitmotif resounded fleetingly, in haste. And that now we . . .?

HELEN: Should begin the opera, you mean? . . .

GEORGE (*nods*): Yes, the plot . . .

HELEN (*smiling*): Why are you changing the words? It would still be just an opera. That's what I was afraid of.

GEORGE: You were?

HELEN: The whole night. (*Pause*)

GEORGE (*begins pacing back and forth*): All this is nonsense. (*Pause, as he continues pacing*) Strange!

HELEN: Yes, George, that's what it is: strange. But we shouldn't let ourselves become confused.

GEORGE *stops*.

HELEN: Yes—for most people do let themselves become confused. If some lively tune makes them dizzy, they try to play it again in everyday life. But what was intended for a dance hardly lends itself to walking. It easily becomes ridiculous and bizarre. And that's not what we want, is it, George? Not with our highly tuned feelings.

GEORGE: You've reflected about all that?

HELEN: I knew you wouldn't do it. I think I'm older than you.

GEORGE *gestures*.

HELEN (*softly*): Not last night . . . then I was . . . well, you know. (*In a different tone of voice*) But . . . at least we know now that we are different people.

GEORGE: Different?

HELEN: And new. Because we were able to have all of that in the midst of a party, totally unconcerned, like two people who can make themselves invisible. . .

GEORGE: You said that yesterday, too: like two people who . . .

HELEN: Yes, wasn't it like that? Just think how much we already have overcome convention . . . It no longer disturbs us. Today they will talk about how the painter Millner paid court to me. Tomorrow, my aunt will tell me that she would be very pleased to meet you, and then she'll wait two weeks to see if you pay us a visit. (*She laughs.*) And meanwhile we have as good as lived together for twenty years. Yesterday, while two hours were passing by for everyone else.

GEORGE: Why precisely twenty years?

HELEN (*gaily*): Well, after all, we died young, didn't we?

GEORGE *shakes his head.*

HELEN: Died in the midst of joy! How beautiful that is! Do you think other people ever have experienced *that?*

GEORGE (*mockingly*): In this way, we could have *many* lives, couldn't we?

HELEN (*seriously*): Yes, don't you see?—That could be the art of modern man.

GEORGE: The art? . . .

HELEN: Or the task: to find the proper rhythm for every experience. Then each one would be complete, a life. And you would live a thousand lives . . .

GEORGE: And die a thousand deaths . . .

HELEN: All of which you would overcome . . . can't you feel it?

GEORGE: How did you arrive at that?

HELEN: At these ideas? Do you have to ask? (*Gets up.*) You're a painter, George. If you paint a picture of an evening, is it *one* evening?

GEORGE: No, of course not. I fuse many similar evenings together in my picture, perhaps all the ones I happen to know.

HELEN: You see, you just revealed the secret yourself.

GEORGE: How so?

HELEN: Did you come straight from work to the dinner last night?

GEORGE: Not exactly . . . but . . .

HELEN: But you would have been able to work? . . .

GEORGE: Yes, I suppose I could have created something.

HELEN (*happily*): And you did. With the measure of a work of art you came upon me and made me complete, made us complete . . . Out of "us" you made a work of art, something eternal . . .

GEORGE (*sadly*): Which today no longer exists.

HELEN: Oh . . . do you think your paintings are *here* . . . I mean, is what you have created here accessible to everyone? No! Only to those who find their way to where your pictures *are*, where they *live*. That's where *we* are too, George—Eternally!—

GEORGE (*looks at her seriously. Pause*): And that's how you arrive at this idea?

HELEN (*nods*): That we found something that is important to life.

GEORGE: But aren't there already many people who—how shall I say—live without following examples, without adapting themselves to tradition, who are like pioneers; they must then quite instinctively apply the proper measure to the individual experience.

HELEN: Yes, subconsciously, they may do that in one, two, or three instances. But they are all still beginners: at most they learn five or six tempos which they then apply to everything . . . But life has thousands of them. And once a mistake is made, they fall into confusion and seize that convention which seems for the moment to come closest to their situation . . . (*Pause*) You, for example, would have married me . . .

GEORGE (*sincere, surprised*): No.

HELEN: Oh no? What would we have done?

GEORGE: We—but this is all nonsense.

HELEN: No, no, please tell me, how did you imagine our future?

GEORGE: Well, we simply would have stayed together.

HELEN: Here?

GEORGE: Here or, better yet, somewhere else—because of your . . . your aunt . . .

HELEN: Oh, I see.

GEORGE: Just like that. Like many artists . . .

HELEN *laughs.*

GEORGE *hesitates, looks at her questioningly.*

HELEN *laughs.*

GEORGE: Well, what are you laughing about?

HELEN: Oh George, that convention has existed for quite some time.

GEORGE:  A convention for that . . . but . . .

HELEN:  Yes, a convention, not within society, but within certain circles . . . Is that any better? I would have begun to dress carelessly . . .

GEORGE *looks at her, speechless; then he laughs, too.*

HELEN (*laughing*):  You see!—And now let me leave, while we're still laughing.

GEORGE (*startled*):  Leave?!

HELEN:  Yes. Just one more thing. You mustn't be sad. And when you think back about us, never think about our fate except in the tempo in which it is beautiful, in which it is a melody . . . Promise me that . . . Don't try to measure it by the standards of everyday life; you'll do it injustice.

GEORGE (*puts his hand in hers. They look at each other. Silence. Then*):  I suppose I want a kind of happiness that . . . (*He lets go of her hand.*)

HELEN:  That keeps better time with life, you mean . . .?

GEORGE (*quickly*):  Yes.

HELEN:  Shall I tell you what I have been thinking ever since I came here?

GEORGE:  Since you came here?

HELEN:  That kind of happiness . . .

GEORGE:  Will come?—

HELEN:  Or is already here around you . . . It seems as if . . . as if . . .

GEORGE:  As if?

HELEN:  As if it already were here, all around you . . .

GEORGE:  When did it arrive?

HELEN (*calmly*):  Quite some time ago. You just didn't notice it. Because it patterns itself so closely to your life—*its* breathing and that of your life are like a single breath. I could be wrong. I really don't know . . . I'm just talking like a woman . . . But consider it . . .

GEORGE *lowers his head.*

HELEN (*quietly moves away from him*):  Consider if there is someone whom you hardly ever have noticed up till now, and yet is always around you. Someone, George, someone whom you cannot separate from life—perhaps . . . Consider it, George

. . . (*Quietly goes to the door, quietly opens it.*) Consider it. (*Exits.*)

GEORGE (*stands there a while, motionless, lost in thought . . . suddenly he starts, like someone awakening from a dream, and looks around him. Gradually he comprehends*): Helen! (*He runs to the door, tears it open and shouts*) Helen!

*He listens, everything remains quiet, then he shuts the door, comes back, paces to and fro deep in thought, takes one thing in his hand, then another. Lights a cigarette. Suddenly he throws it aside, rushes to the table on the right and begins to write rapidly. After a while, he angrily says something incomprehensible, and tears up the sheet of paper. Takes another, begins, writes, stops again. Tears this one up, too. Then he stares off into space, and then with a violent gesture, he buries his head in his hands and remains sitting that way, motionless, with his elbows on the desk. After a while, Mascha comes in very slowly and hesitantly; she keeps looking around shyly. She is carrying a large bouquet of red Italian anemones and a little basket of oranges. When she comes in thus and notices George, who is sitting there motionless with his back to her, she is startled.*

MASCHA (*softly*): Hello.

*Everything remains quiet. She goes silently to the stove, gets an earthenware jug, and, as she carries it to the paint cabinet, she arranges all the bright anemones in it. During all this, George shifts a bit in his chair and observes her. He is about to get up, but then he remains sitting and watches her movements.*

MASCHA (*suddenly senses his gaze. Quickly*): You were asleep. I just brought the flowers. And there are the oranges . . .

GEORGE (*quickly*): Fine, fine. (*Gets up and comes closer.*) You brought anemones? Do you like them?—

MASCHA (*startled*): Aren't they alright?

GEORGE: Oh, yes. (*Takes several blossoms and holds them up to her hair.*) They go well with your blond hair.

MASCHA (*modestly*): Yes, if only the lady is the same shade of blond.

GEORGE (*looks at her in amazement. Then*): Oh—I forgot about that. I was thinking that if we were to make a little wreath out of these anemones and put it in your hair . . .

MASCHA (*touches the anemones*): Would you like to paint that? . . .

GEORGE: Let's assume. I'd like to paint that. You with the little wreath. And it would go so well, just the way I need it, but . . .

MASCHA: But?

GEORGE: But I might not be in the mood to paint just at that moment—or I might have a headache.

MASCHA: Then I would wait.

GEORGE: But in the meantime it will get dark, and the chance to paint is gone for the day.

MASCHA: Well, then maybe it'll work out the next day.

GEORGE: But who would be able to put the wreath back exactly the way it was the first time—

MASCHA: Well, then I would keep on sitting here with the little wreath on my head.

GEORGE: All night?

MASCHA: Yes.

GEORGE: But you mustn't fall asleep. It might move.

MASCHA: Well, then I mustn't fall asleep.

GEORGE: And besides, by morning the flowers will have wilted in your hair . . .

MASCHA (*sadly*): Yes—that's true. And with the wilted wreath . . .

GEORGE (*turning away*): It won't work.

MASCHA: That's right! (*Pause. She continues to arrange the flowers.*) And the lady?

GEORGE (*suddenly stops, stares at Mascha and comes quickly up to her. Puts his hands on her shoulders and turns her around to face him. He tries to find her eyes*): Mascha . . . is it you?

MASCHA *looks at him in amazement.*

GEORGE: You're always here, aren't you, Mascha?

MASCHA *backs away.*

GEORGE: But—you can't understand any of this, Mascha. (*Helplessly*) Look, Mascha, these flowers belong to you . . .

MASCHA *continues to look at him wide-eyed, not understanding.*

GEORGE (*at a loss*): And—and . . . the oranges, too . . . the oranges, let's eat them together, let's—from now on—always eat oranges together . . .

MASCHA (*suddenly, blissfully*): George?

GEORGE (*takes her in his arms*): I'm sorry . . .

MASCHA *buries her face in his chest, while he softly strokes her hair. Suddenly she sobs.*

GEORGE (*softly*): What is it, why are you crying?

MASCHA (*between laughter and tears*): Because I don't have peace of mind just now—the way you'd like . . .

GEORGE (*tenderly*): You . . .

MASCHA: Yes, I'm just not prepared at all—

GEORGE *kneels quietly before her.*

MASCHA (*puts her hands on his eyes. With a mild reproach, while her smile becomes more and more beautiful*): For so long everything was ready for you. And then you choose the wrong time . . .

*Curtain*

# Orphans

*A Play in One Act*

*Characters:*

SEVEN ORPHAN BOYS, *among them*
    THE OLDER BOY, *who knows a good deal*
      *and is a bit older*
    JEROME, *the smallest*
SIX ORPHAN GIRLS
A BLOND NUN
THE OLD GARDENER

*In the garden of an orphanage. Fall. The linden trees along a wide walk grope toward earth with a hundred wilted hands. In the middle of the walk stands a small Gothic chapel with a pointed belfry. Ignoring the gray building, the walk continues past it further into the park, into the darkness, out of which shimmer the bronze foliage of small oaks and the trunks of young birches. Sometimes one might imagine that the sun shines there. But it is one of those dreary gray days, and early in the afternoon.*

*There appear on the walk: The six girls. Two by two. They are leading each other by the hand. They all have on the same gray dresses and blue straw hats, which they have been wearing the whole summer. They are all the same age (around ten or twelve years old). Behind them come the seven boys. Two by two. They all have on gray suits and flat, blue straw hats. They are all near*

*the same age (around twelve years old). With the seventh boy,
little Jerome, walks the young nun. Slowly and quietly they
approach the door of the chapel. The older boy runs ahead of
everyone, is the first to reach the door, pushes against it, while
he holds the massive handle with both hands.*

THE OLDER BOY (*to the others*): Locked!
*The procession stops.*
THE OLDER BOY (*still at the door*): What now?
*They all turn toward the nun.*
THE BLOND NUN: We'll have to go look for the gardener.
THE OLDER BOY (*quickly raising his hand*): Let me!
THE BLOND NUN (*hesitating*): Yes—but . . . No, I want to look
   for him myself. Perhaps he is in the cemetery . . . (*She walks
   to the right; turns back. To the older boy*) You take charge
   while I'm gone, Paul. (*She leaves.*)
THE OLDER BOY *follows her with his eyes.*
THE BOYS AND GIRLS *do likewise. Pause.*
THE OLDER BOY (*bends down to the keyhole of the chapel door.
   After a while*): Oh!
THE BOYS AND GIRLS *look toward him.*
A BOY: Is she in there?
THE OLDER BOY (*still peeking through the keyhole*): All white!
ANOTHER BOY: All white?
THE OLDER BOY: Lights are burning around her.
*The six boys slowly come nearer, only little Jerome remains with
the girls.*
THE OLDER BOY (*still peeking through the keyhole*): Now I can
   see her quite clearly. She has her eyes closed and something's
   in her hand.
ONE OF THE BOYS: In her hand?
THE OLDER BOY (*as before*): A cross made out of something
   white, and three roses.
A GIRL (*softly*): Roses?
ANOTHER GIRL: I want roses, too.
JEROME: There aren't any more, I think.
A GIRL: White roses?
THE OLDER BOY (*as before*): Everything is white all around her.

A GIRL: Oh!

ANOTHER GIRL: Is she very pretty?

THE OLDER BOY (*as before*): She's ugly—all yellow.

*Pause. Then a girl begins to cry. The other girls gather around her and watch her. Little Jerome stays all by himself. The boys are all at the door of the chapel, behind Paul. Pause.*

THE OLDER BOY (*suddenly steps back, turns around, grabs the nearest boy by the shoulder and pulls him to the door*): There, look!

*The shocked boy screams and runs away.*

THE OLDER BOY (*laughs*): Coward!

*None of the boys laughs with him; they all pull back a little from the door.*

THE OLDER BOY (*at the door*): Is *he* ever scared! All of a sudden he's scared of little Betty. (*He wants to pull another boy over.*)

THE OTHER BOY (*fiercely*): Don't!

THE OLDER BOY: Are you scared, too? You were never afraid of little Betty before, were you?

THE OTHER BOY: But now she's dead.

THE BOYS (*nodding*): Yes.

THE OLDER BOY: Well, and a dead person is less than a living one. A dead person can't do anything anymore. He can't eat anything and he can't say anything. He's like a stone. And he's all cold, too.

A BOY: Really?

THE OLDER BOY: Yes, of course, he's all cold.

ANOTHER BOY: Who says?

THE OLDER BOY: I read it in a book: ". . . He reached for her hand, and it was all cold"—it says—and then, everyone knows that . . .

A BOY: That you turn into stone when you're dead?

THE OLDER BOY: You're stupid. You are what you are—flesh. But dead flesh.

ANOTHER BOY: Do you still have hair and eyes and teeth?

THE OLDER BOY: Eyes?—I think so.

ANOTHER BOY: But why don't you keep on living if you haven't lost anything?

THE OLDER BOY: Because you don't have your soul anymore.

A GIRL: Little Betty had a soul, too?

THE OLDER BOY: Everybody has a soul.

ANOTHER BOY: But she was so stupid.

A LITTLE GIRL (*joyfully*): The soul is a little bird.

A BOY: Oh, no! That's not true.

THE LITTLE GIRL (*slowly*): The soul is a little bird.

THE OLDER BOY (*condescendingly*): The soul is a spirit.

THE PREVIOUS BOY (*to the little girl*): You see—a spirit!

THE LITTLE GIRL (*close to tears*): The soul is a little bird . . .

JEROME (*takes the little girl under his protection*): Leave her alone!

THE PREVIOUS BOY: What does this have to do with you, hm? Are you the prefect maybe? You think you're something just because you get to walk with the nun? Hm? I can do whatever I want, you know. (*He shoves the little girl.*) There—you see!

JEROME *shrinks back.*

THE PREVIOUS BOY: You coward!

ANOTHER BOY: Why's his name Jerome anyway? Is he French?!

SEVERAL BOYS (*laughing out loud*): French?!

THE PREVIOUS BOY: Are you French? All Frenchmen are crooks.

JEROME: I'm not French.

ANOTHER BOY: He doesn't even have another name!

*The boys laugh.*

A BOY: You have to have another name. Everybody has two names.

ANOTHER BOY: At least! I have an uncle who even has five.

A GIRL: Is he the Kaiser?

THE OLDER BOY: The Kaiser just has a first name. Kaisers always just have first names. I read it in a history book.

A BOY: Why?

THE OLDER BOY: Very simple. If we didn't have names, you couldn't keep us straight. There are lots of Pauls and Alfreds and a whole pile of Marys. That's why you have to have another name. But there's only one Kaiser. Right? So he doesn't need a second name. You can't take the Kaiser for somebody else.

A BOY: Because he's got a crown!

*Pause.*

A GIRL: Is little Betty's name still Betty now?

THE BOYS (*shouting all at the same time*): Yes—oh yes—no—
well . . .

A BOY (*questioning, to Paul*): What do you say?

THE OLDER BOY: The name of her soul is still Betty, I think. And
the name she's got now, I heard yesterday.

SEVERAL BOYS AND GIRLS: What?

THE OLDER BOY: The gardener told the servant . . .

SEVERAL BOYS AND GIRLS: What?

THE OLDER BOY (*steps closer*): It was strange! A funny word
with lots of A's . . .

ANOTHER BOY: With lots of A's?

*Pause.*

*In the meantime, little Jerome has sneaked up to the door of the
chapel and, standing on tiptoe, is trying to look through the
keyhole. Steps are heard.*

THE OLDER BOY: Shhh. The nun's coming! (*Commands*) Get
back in line. And nobody better say I looked in there!

A BOY: Jerome'll tell for sure.

ANOTHER BOY: Him? (*Pointing toward the door*) He's looking
himself . . .

THE OLDER BOY (*who has just now noticed Jerome*): What do
you think you're doing there? March! Didn't you hear: back
in line? (*He gives the little boy a hard shove toward the
front.*) Do you think I'll let myself be punished on account
of you?

*Slowly from the right comes the old gardener. A small, weather-
beaten old man, his face and hands are like earth and roots. The
keys jangle against his knee.*

THE OLDER BOY (*softly*): Now I know the word with all the A's.
(*Even softer to the other boys*) Cadaver.

A FEW VOICES (*repeat it slowly*): Ca-da-ver . . .

A GIRL: O—oh!

*The old gardener unlocks the chapel. It is completely quiet, and
we can hear every movement of the key. Then the old man opens
the gray door to the inside. Wide. The garden seems to darken
more quickly from the light of the tall, yellow candles which*

*guard the small, white catafalque. The old gardener enters and, hunched over, putters around the bier and remains somewhere in the chapel, invisible in the dark. The blond nun has appeared right behind him. She gets the lines in order. Then she stops among the little ones, near Jerome, who is staring fixedly at the chapel with his eyes wide open.*

THE BLOND NUN (*her voice is golden, clear*): Children! You are going to visit your little sister Betty for the last time. Your little sister is with God, and I believe she has just become an angel. You may say your prayers to her once more so that she will think of you right from the beginning of her heavenly bliss and tell our Heavenly Father how well you know the Lord's Prayer. (*She places herself with Jerome at the head of the group, which moves slowly and hesitatingly along the linden walk to the chapel. She begins*): Our Father . . . (*And interrupts herself, turning to Jerome*) What?—Are you afraid? (*Then again*) Our Father, Who art in Heaven, hallowed be Thy name, Thy—kingdom—come—

*At "hallowed" a few voices begin with "Our Father" and so on. We hear scattered words of the prayer until they are all in the chapel. We can distinguish the children vaguely: One behind the other, they go around the bier and reappear from the other side on the walk, quiet and astonished. There they gather together quietly. The prayer is over. Still inside the chapel, we hear the nun say: "and in the hour of our death . . ."*

SEVERAL VOICES: Amen!

THE BLOND NUN: Amen! (*With Jerome by the hand, she walks from the chapel where the old gardener is snuffing out the candles.*) Actually it's still playtime. A quarter of an hour to go. Do you want to stay in the garden, children?

THE OLDER BOY ALONG WITH OTHERS (*imploring*): Yes! Yes!

THE BLOND NUN: Then I will take the girls home. I'll come and fetch you later. Are you staying, too, Jerome? You shouldn't be out in the night air, you know.

JEROME: I still have to find some flowers today.

THE BLOND NUN: They're probably all dead.

JEROME (*softly*): But Betty still has some . . .

THE BLOND NUN: Yes—she . . . (*To the other boys*) But don't stay when it gets darker. Take them out on the lawn, Paul. And watch them, you hear? Do you want the balls or the hoops?— What are you going to play?

THE OLDER BOY (*hands in his pockets, uncertain*): Oh, anything—

*Two by two, holding hands, the six girls go to the right into the ever-darkening park. The blond nun last. Through the trees the evening glows, cutting the gray into sharp, narrow strips. The seven boys hang back, as if at a loss for what to do. Jerome whispers with one of them. Pause.*

THE OLDER BOY (*loud*): Ugh, I can't stand incense!

FIRST BOY: Now I know why they call it a cadaver.

SECOND BOY: Why?

FIRST BOY: Because it's as pale as old wax.

THIRD BOY: Or chalk . . .

THE OLDER BOY: Or—cheese . . .

THIRD BOY: Would you want to touch it?

THE OLDER BOY: I did!

SEVERAL VOICES: When?

THE OLDER BOY: Just now, going past. "She" (*he means the blond nun*) didn't notice it.

FIRST BOY: On the face?

THE OLDER BOY: On the hand. Like this. (*He makes a tapping motion with his index finger.*)

THIRD BOY (*with admiration*): Really?

FOURTH BOY: You shouldn't have.

FIRST BOY: What was it like?

THE OLDER BOY: Sort of like . . . not like anything at all.

FIRST BOY: Cold?

THE BOY WHO SPOKE WITH JEROME (*aloud, to Jerome*): But! . . .

JEROME *nods.*

THE SAME BOY (*to Jerome*): Should I say it? (*To the others*) He says she isn't really dead.

*Pause.*

THE OLDER BOY AND TWO OTHERS *laugh out loud.*

THE SAME BOY (*embarrassed*): He says . . .

JEROME (*very serious*): No, she's not dead.

*Renewed, stronger laughter.*

THE OLDER BOY (*visibly amused, laughing to the others*): Shhh. (*To Jerome, ironically*) Well, what is she then?

JEROME (*slowly, very seriously*): She is—something different. You can't . . .

*Laughter.*

THE OLDER BOY (*to the boys who laughed*): Be quiet! Let's hear what he has to say. (*He plants his hands on his hips in mocking imitation.*) Alright, Jerome, she's something different, hm?

JEROME (*slowly, lost*): It couldn't happen here.

THE OLDER BOY: What can't happen here? (*To the others*) Shhh!

JEROME (*amid the general silence*): Dying. (*Pause*) There isn't a tall house, or a tower (*pause*) like in town . . . (*Pause. Explaining quickly*) Dying is a terribly tall, ugly, yellow house. And mama had to jump down . . . from way, way up there— into the yard . . . on the stones . . . (*Pause. Taking a breath*) Then you're—dead.

*Pause.*

A BOY: Your mama? . . .

JEROME (*shivering*): Yes, from way up above. (*Pause*)

THE OLDER BOY (*quickly, angrily*): And you're telling us about it?

JEROME *looks at him with large, expressionless eyes.*

THE OLDER BOY (*motioning with his arms*): Ugh! That's a disgrace. I know that for sure. Only really bad people, the worst people die that way! Shame on you! Shame! (*Screaming into Jerome's face*) Your mother killed herself! (*The other children stand around amazed.*)—You haven't told the sister about that. You liar, you! But we have to tell her. You all heard it: His mother killed herself. (*The boys make no show of agreement.*) Ha ha! My little friend, no more good times for you! As soon as the prefect hears about this . . . look out!

A BOY (*curious*): What'll happen?

THE OLDER BOY: The prefect? He'll simply throw him out of here. Into the street. You coward, you won't have a sister there you can make up to. Where are you going to go then, hm?

*Pause.*

JEROME (*full of confidence, softly*): To mama, in Heaven!

THE OLDER BOY (*mockingly*): Heaven! Of course! Heaven! Your mother in Heaven! She'll be sitting pretty in Hell, hear that?

*The other boys step back, horrified.*

JEROME *trembles, turns completely pale and punches the older boy in the face with his fist.*

THE OLDER BOY (*at first surprised, then red with anger, grabs Jerome by his hands and forces him to his knees. Breathless*): Hit me? You puppy, hit me? What? I'll . . . you miserable coward. Try that again. You're trash, you know. You'll always be trash. Try that again, I dare you!

*Contemptuously and with a violent motion he pushes little Jerome away. The little one falls backward and huddles down on his knees.*

THE OLDER BOY (*hoarsely to the others*): Come out on the lawn! Come on!

*The others follow him most willingly, almost reverently.*

THE OLDER BOY (*turns around once more*): And if you really want your mother (*he laughs*) then you'll have to do what she did, or hang yourself on one of the trees here, or jump into the pond—otherwise you'll never get to your mother in—(*ironically*)—Heaven! Remember that!

*Off to the right. The other boys keep close behind him. They don't make a sound, but they move in an exaggerated manner and take very large steps. In the distance Paul's sharp mocking voice can be heard, words like: "What a . . ." Silence. Little Jerome gets up and listens. He tries a few steps to the right, to the left, and finally stops near the front, not knowing what to do. The park is black, and the trees look human. The leaves are falling steadily. We hear a noise in the chapel, the short rapid blows of a hammer. Little Jerome glances shyly toward the door. First, a bit of light seeps out, then the door opens, the light disappears, we hear the key turn in the lock. Out of the shadows, the old gardener drags himself along, hunched over, rootlike, the little coffin on his shoulder. He crosses the walk, then goes deeper into the black park.*

JEROME (*watches him; pause. Then softly*): Hey you!
*The heavy steps of the old man are farther off; high in the tree-
tops the wind rustles.*
JEROME (*runs a few steps toward the back. Louder, imploring*):
Hey you!
*The trees rustle.*
JEROME (*helpless. Softly*): Hey you!
*Pause. He runs after the old man into the black park.*

*Curtain*

# The White Princess

*A Play in One Act, by the Sea*

*Characters:*

THE WHITE PRINCESS
MONNA LARA, *her sister*
OLD AMADEO, *the steward*
TWO MONKS, *in black masks*
MESSENGER

*Setting. Stage Rear: A prince's villa (toward the end of the six-teenth century). Upon an open loggia with five arches, a simple unbroken second level decorated with pilasters. In front, a terrace bordered by statues from which a staircase with wide steps descends to the garden. In the background, behind the villa: the park.*

*Stage Center: The garden—laurel bushes, mulberry trees, and, in the middle, toward the staircase, a walk shaded by plane-trees. Front, left of center stage: a stone bench with pillows and the statue of a multibreasted goddess.*

*Stage Front: A rock beach (with a landing) and the sea, which rolls in from the audience toward the stage with a calm, uniform rhythm. The villa reflects the sky and the expanse of the sea.*

> THE WHITE PRINCESS *is leaning against the stone bench. She is wearing a soft white gown. In her eyes, waiting and anticipation.*

*Pause.*

OLD AMADEO (*in black livery, serious. He bows low.*)
The prince has gone.

THE WHITE PRINCESS *slowly lowers her head.*

*Pause.*

OLD AMADEO
And what is your command?

*Pause.*

THE WHITE PRINCESS (*pensively*)
It is the first time that the prince has left us,
is it not?

OLD AMADEO
The first time since the wedding of Your Highness.

THE WHITE PRINCESS
And that is long ago.

OLD AMADEO
It is eleven years since we adorned the gate
for your reception.

*Pause.*

THE WHITE PRINCESS
We must not think those years are many.
I was a child.

OLD AMADEO
I can remember still;
the wreath seemed much too early for your brow—
    (*he hesitates apprehensively*)
but out of children queens are made . . .

THE WHITE PRINCESS
Yes, when from them every rose is stolen
and every myth,
and ripening orange blossoms
bedeck their brows
till they accept the shadows,
which from the early bridal wreath flow cold:
then out of children—queens.
    (*Pause. She rises, more animated.*)
The prince took many servants to the woods with him?
    (*Quickly*)

Send everyone away and clear the rooms for me,
so none will meet me in the hallways;
I long to feel as if I came today
to sing, to dress the pillars
with vast and heavy clusters
of fruity ornament.

OLD AMADEO

Command me, I will find a pretext
and cast the servants to the winds;
but surely I may tend your day?

THE WHITE PRINCESS

No, you go, too. I think you've long
wanted to see your children's children in Pietrasanta.
Today it shall occur.

OLD AMADEO

You never fail to shower me with kindness . . .

THE WHITE PRINCESS

It is not kindness. It is merely that you give
that very freedom to me in return.
And since you are so fond of Monna Lara,
take her along to see your little ones.

OLD AMADEO

You truly treat me to a treasure there.

THE WHITE PRINCESS

And don't forget: take silks and linens
from my trunks
as much as you are able.

OLD AMADEO

You'll make us rich.

THE WHITE PRINCESS

If only I could rid you of your worries!
For who has time—there is so much to life—
to think of hardship, of the little things,
when great things are awakening within us.
We should not weep, nor should we laugh;
we should float freely like a skiff adrift
and listen to the rhythm of our own deep keel.
    *Pause.*

Forgive me, I have lost myself in thought. You see,
these thoughts have strangely gathered up inside me,
year after year. As one who writes a song,
and one who's very old and then
discovers this and that within.—But go,
when you return, I want to hear things
which will charm a child. Much joy
awaits you. Me, as well, perchance.
Let's think of one another.

> OLD AMADEO *bows low. He goes down the plane-tree walk toward the house and across the terrace.* THE WHITE PRINCESS *walks up to the shore. In her eyes, the sea. She slowly raises her arms and holds them wide-outstretched for a while.*
> *Pause.*

> MONNA LARA *approaches from the terrace. She is wearing a flowing dress of faded blue. Softly she puts her arm around the princess. Both look out to sea.*
> *Pause.*

> MONNA LARA (*softly*)

Let me stay with you.
> *Pause.*

> THE WHITE PRINCESS

But you love children, do you not?

> MONNA LARA

I love you.
> *Short pause.*

> THE WHITE PRINCESS

You don't know who I am.

> MONNA LARA *turns her head and looks into her sister's face.*

> THE WHITE PRINCESS

You child . . .

> MONNA LARA

Are we not sometimes older
in our dreams?
I saw you there. And you were like a tree.
You stood alone, so green with youth,
and you were glowing with the evening's light.

And I went up and came quite near and looked
and said aloud: You have not blossomed yet.
And asked: When will you be in bloom?
      THE WHITE PRINCESS (*takes both of her hands. Softly*)
Imagine now, the dream has not yet passed.
Stay deep in dream, my sleeping sister.
Be it your dream and mine.
If you have often dreamed, you know
how unpredictably dreams shape their course.
They turn, they bolt,
and they are filled with peril.
They run and chase, and then again they stop,
unwilling to go on.
They tremble just as horses tremble,
when from somewhere
quite the same rider nears again.
Quite the same beast, the same master atop,
pale and distorted.
Thus we dream without plan, I feel.
You realize much can happen in a dream.
And it can be completely altered there.
As noiseless as a flower you may fall asleep
and yet awaken with a scream . . .
      MONNA LARA
But dreams are dreams. They come and go.
When morning breaks, the house is light,
and every dream looks different there.
      THE WHITE PRINCESS
And yet are ever woven into us.
Consider, what life is *more* lived
than the events within your dreams? Or more your own?
You sleep alone. The door is locked.
Nothing can happen. And yet, from your reflection
a foreign world flows into you.
   *Pause.*
Often have I lain this way. Outside
were wandering steps, now nearing, now receding;
for me it was the heartbeat of another,

which beat outside and which I felt within.
I felt it as an animal feels death,
but I could not explain just what it was.
Yet mornings they would comb my hair,
and constantly they dressed me for one day—
it seemed to me it was a year.
It was as if my whole life stopped,
as long as I remained awake;
and all that happened tumbled by
into the clutches of my dreams—
but now I know: it is still there.
The world is vast, but grows as deep
within us as the ocean floor.
It matters little if you woke or slept—
you still have borne all that is life,
your sorrow will yet be, and fortune
will yet smile. For when you sleep
necessity emerges through the twilight,
and, with a beaming face, at last your destiny arrives.

    MONNA LARA

I know not, sister, what you mean.
I only see you. I'm in pain because of you.
You weigh on me. And yet I want to know you better.
I want to spend a night upon your pillow.
I want to comb your warm hair in the morning—
three hours—as long as I have strength left in my arm.
I want to serve you.

    THE WHITE PRINCESS

You never seemed so fully grown to me before.

    MONNA LARA

I want to weep with you.

    THE WHITE PRINCESS

I do not weep. My thoughts are with one man.

    MONNA LARA

Can you behold him clearly?
I want so much to think of one myself,
but I'm unable to create his picture,
each image melts so strangely in my sight.

THE WHITE PRINCESS
I feel him more distinctly as the years pass by.
He held your hand once
(you were little then).
You saw him as a shape among huge shapes,
I saw him not my own.
But in one night, that one in which I wept
long, wanting consolation,
amidst my tears his image formed from my own hands.
And since that time it's grown within me
as a young boy grows;
and is a man.

MONNA LARA
Then it can be: that we forget completely
in order to remember all.

THE WHITE PRINCESS
We are a twilighting abyss
of falling, distant things.

MONNA LARA
And my days? And night after night?
And I should wait?—God, how all life
is long and languid.

THE WHITE PRINCESS
Dear little sister, do not fear;
remember, this is all our dream:
what's brief is long there, and what's long
is without end. And time is space.

*She takes Monna Lara's head in her hands and kisses her fore-
head with lasting, tender affection. Old Amadeo, who has been
standing in the walk for a while, approaches cautiously; he
bows.*

OLD AMADEO
Your Highness—

THE WHITE PRINCESS
Have you not left as yet?

OLD AMADEO
Forgive me.
We were ready to depart

when, garbed in dusty clothes, a messenger arrived;
he's waiting in the hall now with a letter.

THE WHITE PRINCESS

I wish to see him.

OLD AMADEO *bows.*

THE WHITE PRINCESS

And Monna Lara will go with you at another time
to pay a visit to your blond grandchildren.

MONNA LARA (*to Amadeo*)

Early on a summer morn we'll ride
to Pietrasanta, you and I;
today, old friend, I'll greet them from afar,
I am too sad and solemn . . .

OLD AMADEO *bows low. Goes into the house.*

MONNA LARA (*smiling thoughtfully*)

Too solemn for children. And yet a child.
Is that not true? What else?
Something is changing, something leaving me.
But what's to come has not as yet begun.
My hands are migrant birds,
that fly across the sea for the first time:
they have no reference points to guide them.
And so they try to blaze the waves
to mark the pathway homeward.

THE WHITE PRINCESS (*takes both her hands and looks at her*)

They think they are alone;
yet flocks fly this route to the burning hills;
the sky rests on a million wings.
And all reach the abundant heat.

*Meanwhile, the messenger has quickly come up the walk; when Monna Lara notices him, she frees herself and looks toward him. Suddenly, as if afraid:*

MONNA LARA

Shall I go in? You wish to be alone?

THE WHITE PRINCESS

No. When you go, it only seems that way.
What does it mean when countless trees move past you.
What you are scarcely moves at all.

You are not gone and I am not alone.
*The messenger approaches the princess and hands her a letter.*
*Then he backs away to the edge of the walk. The princess opens*
*the letter and hands it to Monna Lara without reading it; she*
*smiles.*

THE WHITE PRINCESS

I've known the message for some time. But read.

MONNA LARA (*she reads carefully, as if with effort*)

And if you wave . . . What does this mean?

THE WHITE PRINCESS

That I'm alone. That I am in command.
That he may land his barque here on the beach.
And that I'd strangle anyone
who would betray us: with these hands.

MONNA LARA (*astonished*)

He is to come, today, here, to our shore?
To land here, truly, like a guest?

THE WHITE PRINCESS

Did you not know that?

MONNA LARA

To me it almost seemed
that something would befall us on this day.
(*with sudden admiration*)
How lovely, how wondrous and strong you are.

THE WHITE PRINCESS (*in thought*)

He even sends a letter; such a child.
He must still write me, this beloved lad:
"Behold, I'm coming." . . . Does he think my blood is blind?
*Another* messenger. I have received a hundred
messengers this very day. Fragrance and wind,
song and silence, distant wagonwheels,
a birdcall, and you, your wanting to stay—
what was not a messenger? How many messengers
are standing there before my heart—are ringing in my ear
and throbbing in my veins—oh!
And he is worried that I'd lose him yet.

MONNA LARA

I can imagine that he wishes to be certain.
If something were to happen,

if fate should turn and threaten—
oh, what anxiety is caused by this great nearness
of things to come.

THE WHITE PRINCESS

The messenger.
He's waiting still, and we neglect him.
   (*She beckons. The messenger approaches and bows.*)
You shall have food, my friend. The sun has shone
upon your letter. Your way was long and hot.
You are from Lucca?

MESSENGER

As you say.

THE WHITE PRINCESS

I know.
And how are things in town?

MESSENGER

Your Highness,
the town is gray. Gray as this dust.
It seemed as if no joy could enter there.
The town was without voice, save at the gate
where sentinels were scuffling as I passed;
they yelled and fell out after me.
Thank God that I was spared this skirmish.
I got out unharmed—

   THE WHITE PRINCESS (*sits down on the bench; during the
   following, she pays less and less attention to the words of the
   messenger and withdraws into herself, staring with wide-open
   eyes toward the sea.*)
You journeyed on, I may presume, unharmed
and filled with courage? So you traveled well?

MESSENGER

I traveled well, Your Highness, though
there was but little shade. Still, it was better
than passing through the villages.
To wander through the outcries of their pain
was just like wading through a field of knives.
Death is there, Your Highness, death.
I saw a house, and in the doorway
a pregnant woman screamed and tore her hair.

And many women who were not with child
screamed—out of fear, I think—like her.
And here and there someone walked past me,
and all at once he grabbed I-know-not-what
and bit the air, and suddenly,
a scream erupted through his blue, convulsive lips.
A scream, they say, who lets such things disturb him?
I've heard the screams of many men, indeed,
and I have screamed some in my time as well;
but never have I heard a scream like his.
Yes, there are things a man cannot forget:—
this was the fear one sees in beasts,
the fear of women lying in hard labor,
the fear of little children was there too—
and this fear grabbed the man and threw him down,
as if it were to tear him into pieces.

> MONNA LARA (*who is staring at the messenger, shyly steps back
> to the bench. She forces herself to say*)

Was it in San Terenzo, what you saw?

> MESSENGER

No, noble lady, it was in Vezzano.
In San Terenzo all was quiet.
I stepped into a church and prayed,
there in the single altar's light,
for a safe passage. I was quite alone.
But in Sarzana, in the town's cathedral,
they were singing. Did I say singing? No,
that singing turned into a scream as well:
the organ screamed along with seven hundred voices.
They knelt, young lady. And their necks
were like ripe rhubarb stalks, swollen with sound.
Like gasping mouths, the men's eyes were wide-open;
the women's eyes were shut.
Even the children found no peace:
they stretched their arms like elongated necks
and held them like a second mouth
out of the crowd, out of the frenzied mob;
mercy! they cried out, mercy! And:

mercy! the massive bishop thundered
on the highest altar at the tabernacle,
so that the glistening chalice trembled
and appeared to glance about.
But still they screamed; it was as if the Lord were pulling
the upper notes of their long voices, like long hair.
And as I wedged myself among the others,
I felt (and I still feel it in my bones)
the whole cathedral rise—and fall again,
like one deep breath.—A miracle it was.
And we need miracles. You did not see
how Death goes in and out as if he were in his domain
and it is not *our* kind of death, it is a stranger . . .
a stranger from some godforsaken place,
a death not in the service of our Lord . . .
>    THE WHITE PRINCESS (*suddenly looks up*)
Death? What did he just say?
>    MONNA LARA
I beg you, order him to leave.
The things he's saying make me shudder.
>    MESSENGER
An alien Death, I said, whom no one knows,
but he knows each and every one . . .
>    THE WHITE PRINCESS (*sees Monna Lara's fear*)
Forgive that I've let him continue,
it seemed to me like music from afar.
>    (*She perceives that in her agitation Monna Lara has taken the
>    letter she had all this time and torn it up completely. Smiling*)
And look, my letter . . .
>    MONNA LARA *startled*.
>    THE WHITE PRINCESS (*without reproach*)
Your hands have a life
of their own—
>    (*to the messenger*)
My good friend, many a man is in the steward's house
who'd give your news the heed which it deserves.
Here are but women, unaccustomed to such weighty words.

Be kind enough to spare us now, especially this
child.
   MESSENGER (*steps back and bows*)
Forgive, Your Highness, I was blind
and did not see how it affected the young lady.
My words swept me away, as words can do.
But if you'd give me leave
to say just *one* thing more.
   THE WHITE PRINCESS
If it is gentle, then you may proceed.
   MESSENGER
You are unguarded here. That is not right.
The park is open as Elysium,
and anyone may walk along the beach.
And so I think, forgive me, it could happen
that those curs might come; they are
already roaming quite nearby. I saw
four of these vultures haunting an abode;
they lie in wait with deadly perseverance,
and if you beckon from the window timidly,
they come and carry from the house what's dead therein:
children, men, women—it's the same to them.
I've heard they also look for all the sick;
but *how* they look? God knows,
their faces are not to be seen.
Cold horror issues forth from them.
I could not trust a single one.
Now, what they do may be compassionate and Christian:
they take the corpses, and they carry them away,
as it is proper, yet I wonder
what is it that they carry *into* every house?
And when they stand outside within the fire's glow,
and when the flames rise from their mighty pyres
of smoke and quivering flesh, they drift freely
back and forth through the inferno.
It seems as though the ones who keep on living
are duty-bound to buy their freedom from the brothers.

THE WHITE PRINCESS

You must do that, my friend;
Tomorrow I will send the ransom to you.
Be safe tonight inside the steward's house;
you will be guarded there and you can sleep in peace,
and thus remain protected in the world.
Go in God's name.

MESSENGER

Thank you and pardon, noble ladies,
my rambling on. In these mysterious times,
it helps to talk about how things are going.
Thank you, and don't forget, post guards,
it's best; they stick to you like leeches
and prepare the funeral pile, so you might think
you, too, must sleep upon it.

THE WHITE PRINCESS

Well, for tonight another bed shall warm you still.
I hope you will take comfort and be happy,
let sleep inspire courage for your safe return.

MESSENGER *bows and leaves through the walk.*

MONNA LARA *who has been standing completely transfixed,
suddenly bursts into tears. The princess pulls her down onto
the bench beside her and takes the head of the crying girl into
her arms.*

THE WHITE PRINCESS

My dear child, what perturbs you so?
You must not be afraid. It was but coward's babble,
void of substance, brought about by fear.

MONNA LARA

I did not know all that . . .
Now suddenly it all comes over me,
now it befalls me; until now
I did not see that life is ominous.
That what I've had, this innocent existence,
              was not true life—
Whoever lives, is helpless, sad, and all alone,
alone with worry, fear, peril, and death.

THE WHITE PRINCESS

Supposing it were thus, my dear, you see—
supposing it is, as I've been for years,
do you think I would wish to ban
the days that were so desperate from the melody
of the great happiness I feel today?
The days say: Death—but listen when I say it:
Death—is it not a wholly different kind of sound?
Only one, in isolation, it becomes a frightening thing.
Take all of them together—for your own,
the countless words, and put them into use:—
where they grow into something great, something profound,
only there will that solitary word grow too.

MONNA LARA

But words are not at stake here: they are dying.
They're dying, many of them. Now and now and now.
They're struggling still, they're hopeful till the end;
and when Death's fingers are in readiness to choke
the life from them, they're hopeful, haunted
by their fear.

*Monna Lara looks around helplessly. Silence. The princess shakes her head softly.*

MONNA LARA (*listening attentively*)

And now!

(*She throws herself down at the princess' feet, imploring her with clasped hands.*)

Oh, let us help! Let's fetch soft linens
from your closets for the beds, and all the things
we have prepared for women great with child,
the bandages, shirts, ointments, charms.
The bitter drops and gentle oils,
the medications for their ailing blood—
oh, anything they never had inside their hovels
that works a miracle. Why does no miracle occur?
I wish I knew what words would reach *You*:
Holy Mary! Why will *You* not touch them?
Where are the lips that kissed the Saviour's wounds?
Does this disgust You? Then if *You* won't deign

to work a miracle upon their reeking bodies,
work one on me: Fill my breasts with milk
so I may quench their thirst . . .

> *Monna Lara, still kneeling, thrusts herself back and holds her
> breasts up, as if she were waiting for them to be filled. She
> remains thus for a while; her tension mounts, breaks off, and
> she falls forward onto her sister's lap.*
>
> THE WHITE PRINCESS (*she caresses the hair of the kneeling girl,
> gently, soothingly, and, bending over her, speaks softly but
> urgently*):

We will put our goods to their use. We will smooth the
wrinkles in their beds so they may feel like the children of the
rich. We will speak to them the way we do to animals so
they won't fear us, and so we lose our fear of them as well. I
will lie down with those who are freezing. I will cradle the
heads of the dying. I will wash the old men and spread their
beards out over their blankets. Cheerfully will I look after
the children and relieve their mothers; their blue nails and
their pus will not frighten me away. And I will care for the dead—

> *Pause.*
>
> MONNA LARA *raises her head. She is very quiet, almost
> sober.*
>
> THE WHITE PRINCESS (*looking past her, hesitating*)

Starting tomorrow, this will be the work
of my days—and of my long nights.

> MONNA LARA

Starting tomorrow?

> THE WHITE PRINCESS

Starting tomorrow, sister. Today I am his,
whose arrival is drawing near.
Like his ancestors' legacy I shall be his,
a treasure all his own.
Even my husband saved me for him;
with his excessive, savage temper,
which no one could control when he's enraged,
he held in check the words and ways of others:
the noblemen, the poets, and the Duke.

> *Pause.*

So I remained a bride. Engaged to one so far away.
*Monna Lara has gotten up during these last words; she stands
rigid and helpless, almost puppet-like before the princess and
speaks in a strangely toneless voice.*

MONNA LARA

And your husband, the prince, he never lay with you?
(*Pause. The princess looks out to sea.*)

THE WHITE PRINCESS

He lay with me.
(*She gets up; Monna Lara shrinks away from her.*)
When music soothed him in the evening,
so he desired nothing,
I offered him my bed.
His eyes did dwell on me in thanks,
but his hard lips were mute.
That's how he fell asleep.
And I was not afraid at all.
Sometimes I sat up nights and looked at him,
the furrows deep between his brows,
and then I saw: he dreamt of other women
(perhaps of that blond Loredan, who loved him so)—
but he dreamt not of me. Then I was free.
For hours I looked through high-arched windows past him:
the ocean, like the sky, was wide and without waves,
and something bright, which slowly sank;
which no one sees and says: The moon is setting.
And then an early fishing boat drew by in space
as silent as the setting moon.
The drifting of these two appeared to me connected:
with one the heavens sank toward me;
and with the other the horizon drew away.
And I was free, awake, with no one there to watch me,
initiated to this solitude.
It seemed as if it all were streaming out from me,
and, like a dream, drifted through space.
I stretched, and, as my body moved,
a fragrance seemed to spread from me and touch it all.
And just as flowers give themselves to space,

so every breath of air is laden with their scent—I drifted
willingly into the dream toward my lover.
And for these hours I commanded him.
   *Pause.*
But there were other hours when I lost him.
When I would wake within and *he* stood there outside,
perhaps in readiness to break in through the door—
I was a tomb then: stone beneath my back,
and I myself as hard as sculptured stone.
If an expression showed upon my features
it was but light and shadow from a lamp
upon some senseless chiselmarks.
An image of what I had been, I lay
upon the huge sarcophagus, my bed,
and thus the seconds passed: year after year.
An underneath me in the same position
lay my decomposing corpse.
   (*Pause. Monna Lara approaches the princess and embraces her
   softly.*)
   THE WHITE PRINCESS
Behold, thus there is death in life.
They both run warp and woof,
as threads run through a carpet,
and form an image for a passer-by.
When someone dies, that's not the only kind of death.
Death is: when someone lives and does not know it.
Death is: when someone cannot die at all.
Manifold is death. You cannot bury it.
Birth and death occur within us daily,
and we are merciless like nature which endures
beyond them both, without compassion or concern.
Joy and sorrow are but colors
to the stranger who beholds us.
That's why it means so much to us
to find one who can truly see,
who pieces us together in his vision, simply saying:
I see this and that, where others only guess or lie.

MONNA LARA

Yes, yes, that's it. It must be someone like that,
or else the nameless image weighs too heavy.
   (*Short pause*)
He'll come to you today . . .
   (*Short pause*)
How could you tolerate it for so long?
I can scarcely bear it any longer.
When I imagine that I shall be forced to wander restlessly
for yet another year with uncommitted blood—
neglected arrogantly by my own hair like a child,
alone and blind amidst my fires,
a stranger even to the dogs and as though denied,
so foreign to myself that my hands touch
me like those of a serving-girl:
if I must live another year like that,
then after that one year I'll throw myself
before a servant like a raving fool
and beg him to release me from this torture.
How have you stood it?

THE WHITE PRINCESS

My blood was turgid.
Many times it cried so loud that I awoke,
found myself crying, and I laughed into the silence
and bit my pillow till it tore.
On such a night as this—I still remember—
Christ melted from his ebony cross;
so monstrous was my passion: . . .
His arms outstretched, Christ lay upon me.

MONNA LARA

And yet you had enormous strength left in you.

THE WHITE PRINCESS

It was not strength. Greed, wretched avarice it was,
wherewith I saved up all the fires of each year·
for my belated wedding-day.
Now it is here.
My heart is beating like a thousand drums.
The last sweet sap within my roots

has penetrated me; now I am ripe.
My head is beautiful, and like a wispy cloud,
the earth slips under my light feet.

And I may age tomorrow.
> MONNA LARA

You are young—
> THE WHITE PRINCESS (*smiling tenderly*)

Youth is but the memory
of one who has not yet come.
> (*She grasps her sister's shoulders with both hands.*)

You, too, will save yourself for your bridegroom;
for your impatience is a passing thing.
Life is long.
> *Pause.*

> MONNA LARA (*in admiration*)

You spread a crown of light
and strength as would a queen.
> THE WHITE PRINCESS (*sitting up straight, looks back to-*
> *ward the palace*)

The sun is sinking; it is mirrored on the house.
Now I will wait and later I will wave.
> MONNA LARA

And if you did not wave?
> THE WHITE PRINCESS

It would mean: danger
threatens us.
> MONNA LARA (*with her eyes closed, sad and dreamy*)

He would glide by, from right to left,
just like the early morning fishing boat.
> (*She opens her eyes as if in terror.*)

But you will wave?!
> THE WHITE PRINCESS (*happy*)

When over there the sea grows dark,
I'll stand erect and wave into the setting sun.
The house is empty—
> MONNA LARA

Shh! Did you hear footsteps?

THE WHITE PRINCESS (*listens for a moment*)
No, come to the terrace. From the middle
we can look far out to sea.

*With their arms around each other, they pass slowly through*
*the plane-tree walk. The sea breathes more slowly and heavily.*
*As the princess stops once and looks back, Monna Lara says,*
*like a nursery rhyme:*
You cannot give any linens away
Nor oils nor medication,
You have to think of your own bed today
In blissful expectation.

THE WHITE PRINCESS *nods solemnly as they go on. A bit further,*
*Monna Lara takes the princess by the hand. They both stop,*
*the princess looks out to sea again.*

MONNA LARA
May I prepare your bed for you and go
to fill the basin so that you may bathe your face?
I feel as though my hands would know
the very things that you will need today.

(*The princess nods, and they go on; they come to the terrace*
*steps and stop again.*)

MONNA LARA (*suddenly kneels down*)
I will prepare your bed; I want to serve you.
All I am I give to you—

*The white princess gently helps her up, takes her head in her*
*hands, and looks into her eyes.*

THE WHITE PRINCESS
Your eyes are vast and new.
I see my happiness in them.

*She kisses Monna Lara on the mouth. Monna Lara breaks away*
*quickly and runs into the house. Now the princess ascends the*
*last steps, turns and looks out to sea in great anticipation. After*
*a while, Monna Lara appears carrying a silver mirror, which,*
*as she kneels, she holds up to the princess. The princess slowly*
*arranges her thick hair.*

MONNA LARA (*beneath the mirror, softly*)
Now he has reappeared within me.

Once he took me by the hand.
And in my hand I sense it once again.
I knew him after all, you see . . .
> *The princess smiles into the mirror, scarcely hearing. There-*
> *upon she rises and gazes into the distance.*

MONNA LARA

Now the sun is sinking in the sea.
(*She hurries back into the house.*)
*Pause.*

*Now the White Princess stands on the terrace alone, looking out*
*erect and intent. Behind her the villa grows brighter and*
*brighter (as if festivities were glowing inside) from the reflec-*
*tion of the setting sun. Then the princess sees something, off*
*to the right, far away. She reaches once in the direction of her*
*sash pocket as if getting ready to wave. Then she waits. Now*
*the sound of oars is heard; they come closer. While the princess*
*follows the movement with her whole body, a brother of the*
*Misericordia has come along the beach from the right (from*
*the point of view of the audience); he is wearing a black mask*
*over his face. The brother has gone up to the beginning of the*
*walk. A second one follows him. They look at the house and*
*whisper. Now, as the princess quickly reaches for her pocket,*
*they both start moving, and the first monk takes several quick*
*steps forward. Then he hesitates, turns back to his companion,*
*and stops. The White Princess has seen him. From this moment*
*on, she sees only him; her body is petrified with terror, she*
*loses the sea from sight, from her consciousness, while now the*
*beating of the oars is loud, slow, hesitating. The princess makes*
*a tremendous effort to break the terrifying spell, to wave in*
*spite of it. This struggle lasts a while. During one of her*
*ponderous, painful movements, the second brother takes a few*
*steps so that he is standing on the walk, almost alongside the*
*first. The princess is motionless. The front of the villa begins*
*to darken. The boat must have sailed past; softly, more and*
*more distant, the sound of oars is lost in the heavy surge of the*
*nearly nocturnal sea. Then, just barely discernible, up in the*
*house the curtain of one of the high bay windows is pulled back,*

*and something bright and slender appears, almost like the figure of a child, and waves. Waves, first beckoning; stops a moment and waves differently: ponderously and slowly, with lingering gestures, the way one waves good-bye.*

*Curtain*

# APPENDIX I

## History of Publication and Performance

The following is a list of the plays in this volume with references to the time of composition, publication, and performance. All plays appear in Ernst Zinn's six-volume edition of Rilke's *Sämtliche Werke*, Wiesbaden, 1959 (henceforth referred to as *SW*). Original titles, where different, are given in parentheses.

MURILLO, probably written 1894; first published in *Psychodramen-welt*, 1 January 1895; *SW* III, pp. 97–100; no known performance.

"NOW AND IN THE HOUR OF OUR DEATH. . . ." (*"Jetzt und in der Stunde unseres Absterbens. . . ."*), probably written 1895–96; first published in *Wegwarten* II, 1 April 1896; reprinted in F.A. Hünich, *Aus der Frühzeit Rainer Maria Rilkes*, Leipzig, 1921; *SW* IV, pp. 775–96; performed 6 August 1896, in Prague.

EARLY FROST (*Im Frühfrost*), written 1895; stage script 1897, Vienna; reprinted in Hünich; *SW* IV, pp. 707–73; performed by a Berlin ensemble (including Max Reinhardt) 20 July 1897, in Prague.

AIR AT HIGH ALTITUDE (*Höhenluft*), probably written 1897; *SW* IV, pp. 813–27; student performance in English, 9 and 10 May 1969, at the University of Arkansas, Fayetteville, Arkansas.

VIGILS (*Vigilien*), probably written 1896–97; *SW* VI, pp. 1249–65; no known performance.

NOT PRESENT (*Ohne Gegenwart*), probably written 1897–98; stage edition 1898, Berlin; reprinted in Hünich; *SW* IV, pp. 829–66; Berlin performance, planned for November 1900, never took place.

EVERYDAY LIFE (*Das tägliche Leben*), written 1900; first published 1902, Munich; *SW* IV, pp. 877–918; performed 20 December 1901, in Berlin; 1907, Breslau; 1936, over Leipzig radio; 1937, Weimar and Munich.

ORPHANS (*Waisenkinder*), probably written 1901; first published in *Revue Franco-Allemande*, vol. 53, May 1901; *SW* IV, pp. 919–931; no known performance.

THE WHITE PRINCESS (*Die weiße Fürstin*), second version, written 1904; first published in Rainer Maria Rilke, *Die frühen Gedichte*, Leipzig, 1909; reprinted separately in Berlin-Steglitz, 1920; *SW* I, pp. 201–31; performed 17 January 1937, in Giessen; student performance in English, 17 April 1970, at the University of Arkansas, Fayetteville, Arkansas.

# APPENDIX II

## *A Guide to Secondary Literature in English*

Rilke's plays have received greater attention from scholars in the United States and Great Britain than elsewhere. The three most detailed studies are theses for the Ph.D. (Roman, Locke) or M.A. (DiNapoli); these, unfortunately, have remained unpublished and are accessible in manuscript form only. All items included in this list illuminate (in part or whole) Rilke's dramatic efforts. Works that do not substantially go beyond a mere reference to the title of a play are not included.

Butler, Eliza Marian. *Rainer Maria Rilke*. (Cambridge: University Press, 1941. Repr. 1946).

DiNapoli, Thomas J. "Rainer Maria Rilke and the Theater." (Master's thesis, University of Texas, 1968).

Locke, John R. "The Plays of Rainer Maria Rilke." (Doctoral dissertation, University of Iowa, 1973).

Roman, Howard. *Rilke and the Theater*. (Doctoral dissertation, Harvard University Press, 1942).

———. "Rilke's Dramas. An Annotated List," *Germanic Review* 18 (1943), 202–8.

———. "Rilke's Psychodramas," *Journal of English and Germanic Philology* 43 (1944), 402–410.

Wood, Frank H. "Rilke and the Theater," *Monatshefte* 43 (1951), 15–26.